GET ONLINE NOW - SETUP SHOP THIS WEEK - ENHANCE THE ONLINE STORE

Your Checklist:

- *get online with a* Miva® **merchant**™ *enabled host*

- *learn Miva Merchant using step-by-step instructions*

- *use Miva and third-party modules to enhance your store's look and functionality*

- *test your online store*

- *open your store to the public*

- *run regular tests and maintenance to keep your store in tip-top shape*

With this book, Miva Merchant and third-party features, you can start today and be ready to go next week!

Use tools to customize your online store - quickly, efficiently and inexpensively. Learn how to build offline, then publish it live.

USE THE BONUS CD FOR FREE PLUG-INS, FREE TRIAL OFFERS, LEARNING GUIDES, REFERENCES AND DEMOS!

Leading Miva Business Partners have offered up more than $1,000 worth of product that will make your online store stand out above the rest.

- A Licensed copy of the OpenUI (a $40 value) for compiled Miva Merchant 4 (versions 4.14 and higher)
- Free Miva Merchant modules
- Demonstration Miva Merchant modules and popular software - try before you buy!
- Guide to using Miva Mia for offline management
- Interactive Catalog of third-party modules
- Special offers and discounts on real solutions
- Profiles on top Miva Merchant online stores
- E-commerce & development resources

New to Miva Merchant? Try it today for 30-Days...totally risk free!

Use the CD keycode to get a 30-day free hosting trial from a Miva Hosting Partner.

Need Support?

MvCommerce.net is the place to go for support on topics in this book. First-time book purchasers also get access to download free update documentations for at least a year. When new Miva Merchant features are added, you'll be the first to get information on them, and how to use them. All at no additional charge.

Get Started Today...

...and when you're ready to really delve in, see the last page for information on using the Bonus CD.

E-commerce
MADE EASY
The *Official* Guide to Miva Merchant

Pamela Hazelton

E-commerce Made Easy
The *Official* Guide to Miva Merchant

Published by
Media Services Int'l Inc
P O Box 827
Clifton Park, NY 12065
www.designextend.com

ISBN: 0-9726604-7-X

Printed in the United States of America

10 9 8 7 6 5 4 3 2 1

This publication has been authorized by Miva Corp.

LIMIT OF LIABILITY and DISCLAIMER: *While the Publisher and Author have used their best efforts in preparing this book, no representations or warranties with respect to the accuracy or completeness of the contents of this book are made. Any implied warranties of merchantability or fitness for particular purposes are specifically disclaimed. No warranty may be created nor assumed or extended by any sales representatives or written sales materials or advertising. The advice contained herein may not be suitable for all situations. Readers are advised to consult with a professional whenever appropriate. Neither the Publisher nor the Author shall be held liable for any loss of profit, time or any other commercial damages, including but not limited to special, incidental, consequential or other damages.*

For information on our products and services, or to obtain technical support, please use the web site supporting this book at www.MvCommerce.net.

Retailers and wholesalers, and companies in need of multiple copies, please inquire our sales department by calling 1-800-967-6744 in the US, or (518) 270-1616.

This book has also been published in an electronic format. Some content appearing in print may not be available in electronic format, and vice versa.

Trademarks: Miva Engine, Miva Virtual Machine, Miva Empresa, Miva Mia, Miva Merchant, Miva Merchant Pro, Miva Merchant Limited Source Kit, Miva Script Compiler, Miva Synchro, Miva Galleria, Miva Warehouse, Miva Conference, Miva Payment, Miva Marketplace, Miva Mailer, Miva Service Club, "We're dedicated to your success in online business." "The Document IS The Application," "High Velocity E-Commerce," htmlscript, and the Miva Corp. "blades..." logo are all trademarks of Miva Corporation, a FindWhat.com Company.

All other trademarks are the property of their respective owners.

Cover design by Mabel Herrera

Preface...

Welcome to the world of *etail*. You're about to enter one of the most exciting, yet sometimes nerve-racking, fields. E-commerce continues to steadily grow—despite market conditions—and will continue to do so over the next several years.

With the stiff competition and escalated costs of operating a brick-and-mortar store, it's no wonder so many companies and individuals are moving to the World Wide Web platform of doing business. While an online store carries its own set of proprietary expenses, it is, in most cases, less expensive than running brick and mortar stores.

Just opening shop online, however, isn't enough. Thousands of new online ventures pop up every month. People and companies have spent their savings and loans, ready to become the next "hot shop" that can do nothing but succeed. It's a good attitude. Even still, more online businesses fail than succeed in their first year, and it usually boils down to poor management.

Don't let the statistics scare you though, because those who succeed do so for very many reasons. Despite what others might say, it's not always because there are millions of expendable dollars to keep them afloat while they make their mark. Successful e-commerce is about more than just money. It's about more than just the products you carry and the audience to which you cater. It's about commitment, time, originality, flexibility, and compromise.

Miva Merchant helps potential and even current *etailers* pave the path for a better future. It is, by far, the most cost-effective online store software on the market. It's simple enough that the most basic Mom and Pop can setup shop, yet expandable enough to be used by the big dogs.

This book is a tool to help pave that path for advancement. There will be no more scratching heads, wondering how you'll display 5,000 products without hiring a construction company. It will help you build and maintain an effective ecommerce site using Miva Merchant.

This book focuses on ecommerce development and Miva Merchant's most recent features. It also focuses on the essential information you'll need to setup shop from scratch. Your success depends on both factors.

This book was written for both newbies and those who are looking to implement a more affordable and customizable package. **If you can click a mouse on a Web page, you can use Miva Merchant.** If you've shopped online before, you can create a custom, highly appreciated Web store.

Best of all, you're going to find out that the myth about spending $30,000 to get Online is just that—*a myth*. With the right knowledge and a strong will to survive this ever-growing, competitive market, just about anyone can shine online. And you won't even have to refinance your house.

So site back, grab a cup of your favorite beverage, and relax. You're about to embark on the wonderful world of ecommerce. This book and Miva Merchant are going to take you there.

About the Author...

Pamela Hazelton has authored several training manuals and tutorials for private and government organizations about various applications, including Microsoft Word, Microsoft Excel, cc:Mail and Photoshop. She has also developed training materials for courses during the first release of Windows 95 (used at Merrill Lynch in NYC), HTML (The Learning Factory), as well as web and print design.

Pamela has provided hands-on computer application and design training for The Learning Factory, CompuTech International, the USPS (via Wang Government Services), and Computer Generated Solutions, along with scores of other corporate and private clients.

Pamela is owner and president of Media Services International, Inc., a web and print design, consulting and representation corporation. Corporate clients include Arts Weekly, Inc., SCOTTeVEST, 2BeadOrNot2Bead, Cemetery Dance, and Weird New Jersey. MSI works with thousands of clients, from startup companies to competing corporations through the company's Miva Merchant customization and design service, DesignExtend.com

Pamela currently resides in Florida with her husband, author Joe Monks, their red-beagle, Luna, and two black cats, Midnite and Shadow, as well as tons of geckos that force their way into the home. She spends her spare time (spare meaning little) writing fiction, cooking and nervously watching her husband and/or the neighbor's kids jump on the trampoline in the back yard.

Pamela's most recent writing venture in the world of ecommerce is an ebook entitled ***Making the BEST of Your Online Store***. The guide was designed to provide analysis training to e-commerce owners, developers and designers.

You can find Pamela through DesignExtend.com, various Miva Merchant user groups and message boards, and at the host site for updates to this book and other Miva Merchant documentation, **MvCommerce.net**. Inquiries about steps in this book can be emailed to: author@mvcommerce.net.

Acknowledgements

When Miva Merchant version 2.0 was introduced, I took some time off to write a tutorial that covered all the aspects of the Administrative interface. That tutorial, totaling nearly 200 pages, was sent to Miva Corp., who gave me the go ahead to offer it as an ebook at my company's Web site, www.designextend.com.

The tutorial, entitled *A Beginner's Guide to Miva Merchant*, was well received, and after a few months, I relaxed, knowing that the 100+ hours I spent delving into every feature and documenting its usage was time well spent. When version 3.0 was released, it was another 50 hours, and when version 4.0 was released, another 50, plus another 75 hours to rewrite the whole thing to be published as an actual book (released by Wordware in 2002).

Earlier this year, the rights to *The Official Guide to Miva Merchant 4.x* reverted back to me, and I set out, once again, to spend another hundred + hours fleshing out what you are now holding in your hands.

I am the author of this book. My colleagues, Miva Corp., and users of Miva Merchant acknowledge this. Just as a movie, however, there are several folks in the background who will never receive the amount of credit they are truly due. Without them, this book wouldn't exist.

I must first thank Miva Corporation, and the many support and executive staff who have been readily available to answer questions and look over the many, many revisions the book has gone through. Miva Corp. has continuously embraced my ideas and the evolution of this as a training mechanism and is kind enough to let me show it off at each year's Miva Conference. When I was under the gun to wrap up this edition, Derek Finley-without hesitation-handed Jimmy Cooper and Linda Eskin over to help me take it through yet another edit. Jimmy and Linda were at my beck and call, and for that I am eternally grateful.

Many of my Miva buddies spent countless hours doing anything they could to help this publication become a reality. All they asked for in return was a signed copy-a very, very small price to pay for their expertise.

Developer Luray Williams has, through every rendition, provided great insight on explaining more complicated lessons to new users. Luray hopped on the bandwagon for the book from the start (back at version 2.0) and has never complained about me sending yet another rewrite for him to go over at 2 a.m. (though he has wondered when he's gonna get that homemade bread I keep promising to overnight to him). Bruce Golub, of PhosphorMedia, jumped in during the final hours to help me tweak some explanations. Both these guys deal with Miva Merchant users every day, so they knew firsthand what to look for.

Miva Developers William Weiland, Adam Denning, Michael Brock, Jonathan Wray, Darren Ehlers, James Harrell, Ivo Truxa, Keith Hunniford, and many others have offered up advice and recommendations through the years and have lent vast amounts of support, including shoulders to cry on when something just wasn't going right. Most of these guys are my competitors in the module sales area, yet we've always found a way to put that aside and just be there for each other. In all my years of business, I've never experienced such a willingness to work *with* rather than against.

Miva Merchant users themselves have played a huge role in the direction this venture has taken, simply by posting questions and answers to user groups. So to anyone who has posted messages since the birth of Miva Merchant, thanks!

Then there's my family and friends, who made themselves available to test the clarity of this book. My father, Robert Hazelton, was the first guinea pig way back when, followed by my sister, Brenda Burton, then friends Al Iriberri and George Bancroft (formerly of Miva Corp.).

It would be horribly selfish of me not to mention those who stood by me, from day one. My parents, Fran and Robert, supported my decision to work for myself, even though I had less than $200 in the bank at the time. Teckla Cooper, my "other" Mom who lived across the street-may she rest in peace knowing that the old-school values she instilled in me gave me the power to get the job done. And my new in-laws, Joe and Nilda Monks, are as supportive as anyone else could be.

The household pets, Luna (the wonder-beagle), and the black cats, Midnite and Shadow, have tolerated the closed office door into the late evening. I don't care what anyone says, animal companions can, and do, nag for attention as much as children.

My assistant and best friend, Judy Miazga has been a huge rock these past months. If something went amiss, she heard about it, and saddled her horse to go to town and fix it. They say not to work too closely with friends and family, somehow I lucked out.

Last, but not least, there's my husband, Joe, who may not realize he is my actual inspiration to take on the huge challenge of finally doing a real book, myself. We were together nearly 8 years before he lost his sight, and we married this past June. It was Joe's drive to not let his blindness force him to live in a dark world of nothingness that made me realize that every single thing we do in life-everything we try to accomplish-is a risk, a crap-shoot. Sometimes we make it, sometimes we don't. If we don't try, we'll never know. My husband believes enough in my work to wager our savings for a house—money we earned because of Miva Merchant.

I'm sure there are scores of folk I've failed to mention. I hope my actions have spoken my thanks for all your help. If not, drop me a line as a kick in the head.

Table of Contents

Introduction to Miva Merchant & References

What is Miva Merchant™?

We could begin by talking code, telling you that Miva Merchant uses a scripting language that varies from HTML and various other languages. It won't make much of a difference, however, because at this point, you're probably just starting out. Either that, or you've finally decided to really understand how to use the administration area of the store you've had running for the past six months.

In a nutshell, Miva Merchant is an online shopping cart that is installed on your hosting company's server. It allows you to sell products, and it allows your customers to not only browse for items by categories or lists, but also search for those products. Essentially, it does what a lot of other shopping cart programs do, only way better. While you might have heard that Miva Script itself is difficult to learn, you don't need to know a thing about the language in order to setup your online store. In fact, you don't really need to understand much of anything. If you can click a mouse and navigate a Web site, you can setup shop using Miva Merchant.

In comparison to dozens of other online store packages, Miva Merchant is actually easier, and better, than most any other shopping cart program out there. Here's why:

- ◆ Miva Merchant can be installed on UNIX or NT servers. Most others may be installed on one or the other, but usually not both.

- ◆ Miva Merchant has a complete administration interface. Therefore, using Miva Merchant "out of the box," actually requires no programming skills whatsoever.

- ◆ Miva Merchant can be customized beyond the depths of most other programs. Hundreds of add-ons exist to make just about anything possible.

- ◆ Miva Merchant isn't restrictive on design. You can change the layout of your store completely, and even add options to products and offer teaser products during checkout.

- ◆ Miva Merchant is inexpensive compared to other carts and the time spent working on them. Sure, you can download some free shopping carts off the web, but good luck learning just how to use them—they often provide scarce documentation and little to no technical support. And what about those $20,000 to start custom solutions? There are many Miva Merchant stores that outdo some of the overblown big sites without totally reinventing the wheel.

- ◆ You can administer a shopping mall, containing dozens of individual stores, each with their own theme and functionality.

- ◆ You don't have to marry anyone. Many existing *etailers* switch to Miva Merchant because they're tired of having to pay a single developer to "unlock" or add features at high costs.

The list does go on. As you continue to learn how to use and administer Miva Merchant, you'll find that its capabilities surpass other programs. You'll be what we call a "Miva Merchant Junkie."

Whom This Book is For

We'll be honest. If you've been using Miva Merchant since version 1.x and have the ability to solve everyone's problems in relation to the operation and administration of Miva Merchant stores, then this book is not for you. Use it as a coaster. We won't be offended. We hope everyone gets to the point where they can finally shelve this documentation and move on to bigger and better things.

However, if you ever find yourself scratching your head, trying to understand how to assign attributes and virtually build your online store, then you've picked up the right tool. With this book, your computer, your own licensed copy of Miva Merchant, and a highlighter, you can build your online store in less than a week. Even better, you'll understand how you made such a fine-looking commerce site, and you'll be begging to do more. Well, maybe not begging, but you will certainly have made a fine accomplishment!

As you learn Miva Merchant, feel free to write in the margins, underline, comment and highlight. After all, it's your book! Circle questions, draw funny faces, even drool on the pages. Taking notes will help in your quest to learn and understand Miva Merchant.

Seasoned users will find this book useful when needing a refresher on accomplishing tasks scarcely done. Many developers use this book as reference when working on client stores, and for explaining certain processes to others.

Versions Covered

This book puts focus on Miva Merchant versions 4.14 and above, otherwise referenced as compiled merchant. In 2003, Miva Corporation restructured Miva Merchant and compiled the source files to make the software run faster, and to offer more protection for the developers of the software.

The most common versions of Miva Merchant running today are versions 4.14 and above (compiled) and versions 4.0-4.13 (uncompiled). As of August 2004, the most recent version was 4.23.

Previous Versions
Users of versions 2.0 - 2.2 and 3.x may also benefit from this book. Features proprietary to version 4.x have been noted as such so version 2.x and 3.x users may continue use of this manual after upgrading to 4.x.

Future Versions
Miva Corp. has already announced version 5. First registered users of each copy of this book are able to download documentation on new features as they become available, for a period of at least one year. This way you will always have documentation to address all the tasks for the version of Miva Merchant you may be running.

What You'll Need

Besides this book and your own ideas, there are a few things you'll need to get started.

A Highlighting Marker

You'll want to take notes and highlight examples throughout this book. This is a tool, not a classic novel, so don't be afraid to make your own markings. *But won't it devalue my book?* Probably, but what's more important—getting a few bucks back later, or saving yourself hundreds of hours hunting for resources?

A Licensed Copy of Miva Merchant

You can obtain use of Miva Merchant through a participating hosting company (found at http://www.miva.com) or, you can purchase a full license from Miva Corp. or one of it's Certified Business Partners.

> *Why purchase a full license? If you are running your own dedicated server you will need a full license. A full license also allows you to carry the existing software with you should you change hosting companies.*

A Domain Name

The domain is the URL (web address) Internet users will type in their browser to get to your site. It's a locator—just like your street address and zip code. If you have a physical store, then you probably already know what you'll call your online store. Ideally, the domain of the store should be exactly or similar to the actual name of the store.

If you don't yet have a name, take the time to you need to think about what best describes your business.

The most favorable domain names end in .com and .net, but other extensions like .biz and .cc are also available. If you reside in a foreign country, there's probably a country-specific domain extension (in Canada it is .ca). Thus, if your name isn't available in .com, you can consider other extensions. If the name you want isn't available at all, or if you only want to use the .com or .net extensions, then you'll need to think of variations.

> *You can check the availability of a domain name at most hosting company and domain registration sites.*

The minute you decide on a domain name, you need to secure it. Domains are registered. You do not "own" the name per se, it is merely registered to you. Once it is registered to you, it is yours to use indefinitely as long as you pay the fees and so long as it doesn't infringe on someone's trademark or copyright (losing it to this would most likely require legal action taken by another party). For example, you should not register domains that are the same as a well-known trademark.

Domain registration costs depend on the extension and the service you use to register them. Some registrars charge $35 per year, while others charge $15. Regardless of the cost, the domain name you select can very well be priceless to your business.

Don't be afraid to register several domains. You can use a main domain for the address of your online store, then "forward" other domains right into it.

Important: Even if you are not entirely sure of the domain you want, once you start leaning toward one, secure it without hesitation. It could be gone tomorrow.

Some Legal Information

If all you plan to do in the next few days is toy with Miva Merchant and get to know it, that's fine. If you're setting up a live store now, make sure you have already researched federal, state and local laws pertaining to your type of business.

If you have a brick and mortar store or a similar business you may already be familiar with the legalities. Just don't guess. Most states have varying guidelines for online company operations.

Some questions you need to have answered are:

♦ Do I need to fill out any special registration forms?

♦ Am I required to collect Sales Tax? If so, how do I do so?

♦ Does my state have any specific return policy guidelines?

If you're a total beginner, you'll need to start at the very beginning—setting up a company, filing registrations for tax ID numbers, and getting detailed information about local laws.

It is vital that you understand what rules you need to follow. You can start by calling a local Chamber of Commerce or City Hall office for information. After you understand the local laws, contact state offices to understand what other regulations will be set on your business.

A Budget

Just as everything you do in life costs money, setting up shop online is no different. From phone costs to shipping to order fulfillment, you need to determine what it's going to cost to run a basic, simple store, and how much you can really afford to spend.

Many people tend to believe they can set up an online store, sell, and fly by the seat of their pants. These stores most always stay very small, or close down within a year.

There are two categories of costs you need to budget. We'll call them direct costs and supporting costs. Supporting costs encompass everything else you need in order to support the operations of the online store.

Direct Costs:

♦ Ecommerce software (Miva Merchant)
♦ Minimum but legally required enhancements (according to laws)
♦ Development of a Web site template
♦ Domain registration
♦ Legal registrations
♦ Order Fulfillment (employees, fulfillment house)
♦ Security certificate
♦ Miva Merchant Add-ons (software that enhances the design or functionality of the store

Supporting Costs:

♦ Telephone (customer service, support)
♦ Email
♦ Postage
♦ Advertising
♦ Printing of invoices, ad material or catalogs
♦ Reliability seals (BBB, etc)
♦ Customer service and support (time and documentation)
♦ Returns and exchanges (also consider the time spent)

These are all very basic, yet often overlooked costs needed to run a business online. The goal is to get an idea of what it will cost to run a simple, out-of-the-box, Miva Merchant store.

A Creative Mind

The possibilities of a Miva Merchant store are virtually endless, giving you the ability to be as simplistic or as extravagant as you can imagine.

References

As you move throughout this book, you'll become familiar with terms and images you'll encounter on the Miva Merchant administration screens and in the actual store you are creating. You'll also become familiar with common terms used for ecommerce.

Common Terms

Every profession has them, and you will know them when you finish building your online store.

HTML (Hypertext Markup Language)—the language used for writing standard pages that are displayed by an Internet browser, such as Internet Explorer and Netscape. The code is translated by the browser to display pages of text and images to the visitor of the page.

Miva Script™—Miva Corporation's own coding language. Unlike many other languages, Miva Script is translated on the server side, so virtually anyone with access to the Web can view pages created via this language.

FTP (File Transfer Protocol) —the method by which you upload graphics and files to your web site and online store.

Some hosting providers do not allow FTP. If you plan to offer many products and eventually have several modifications performed, then you should contact your host and ask them to allow you to FTP to your site. Some hosts will only let you use a Secure Shell connection.

Link (hyperlink) —the underlined text you click on in an HTML page, or in the Admin area for your store, which takes you to a different page or screen.

Module—a file that "plugs in" to the Miva Merchant store to add functionality. For example, in order to configure shipping differently than what is included with Miva Merchant, you may need to install a module that calculates shipping costs in a different way.

Terms We Use

In order to be consistent, and to present information in a way you understand, we will use the following terms when explaining different areas of the Miva Merchant administrative area and the online store (what shoppers see).

Front end—this encompasses the entire store that a visitor sees when they visit your site. It includes the storefront, category pages, product pages, checkout pages, etc. Anything a potential customer sees is on the front end.

Admin—the administration area of Miva Merchant This is where you add products and configure features.

Admin Menu—the left-hand menu of the Admin, where you'll find all the core features you can implement.

Miva Merchant User (also merchant)—the person who is working on the Miva Merchant store using the Miva Merchant Admin.

Potential Customer (or visitor, customer, shopper)—a person who is navigating the online store.

Our Little Icons

To make navigation and an understanding of features easier on you, we've devised some icons. These will assist you in understanding different types of features, as well as version-specific features.

Version Specific Icons

Because new features are commonly introduced in each new release of Miva Merchant, the following icons are used to denote features only available in certain versions. Features are rarely removed. If you are unable to see a feature discussed in this book, check the version of Miva Merchant you are running.

 This icon denotes version 4.x (version 4.00 and higher). It is used to mark features that users of prior versions won't have available to them.

 This icon denotes Miva Merchant versions 4.14 and higher, also known as compiled Miva Merchant. Users of versions 4.13 and lower will not have these features available to them.

Documentation Icons

The following icons are used to alert you to notes, important information and quick tips.

 NOTE—this icon represents a sideline issue we want to make you aware of. Notes in **bold** type are important to how Miva Merchant works and the results you may receive. Notes in *italics* are notes that refer to more optional issues.

 TIP—this icon represents a tip we offer.

 CRITICAL—This icon represents information that is critical, such as problems that can occur and things you should not do at any cost.

W **WIZARD AVAILABLE**—This icon tells you that a Wizard (a more foolproof, but often limited, method) is available to carry out the task.

Miva Merchant Admin Buttons

As you move throughout the Admin area, you'll find several buttons (small graphics) which will assist you in implementing tasks. Get to know them well.

 Holding your mouse over any of the standard Miva Merchant admin buttons will reveal what the button is for.

BUTTON	FUNCTION	FILE NAME
All	Displays all listings, such as products and customers.	all.gif
Assigned	Display only items which are assigned to that category or group (products, customers…)	assign.gif
Unassigned	Display only items which are not assigned to that category or group (products, customers…)	unassgn.gif
Uncategorized	Displays all products which have not been assigned to any category.	uncat.gif
•	Will appear next to a link in the admin area. No drop-down options available.	dot.gif
▶	Signifies that the drop-down list is selected and being viewed.	down.gif
▼	Signifies that more options or listings are available. Located in the main menu.	right.gif
✓	Signifies items which are selected/completed.	check.gif
▣	Launches a color palette for links, background and list.	color.gif
▣	Allows you to create a new item, such as category, product or customer.	new.gif
▣	Allows you to edit the existing item, such as product, category, customer or attribute.	edit.gif
▣	Allows you to edit the item without launching a new screen. Only the information shown on the line can be edited. Note the difference – there is no arrow on this button.	edith.gif
▣	Selects an item.	select.gif
▣	Uploads a file to the store, such as an image or flat file.	upload.gif
▣	Allows you to search for a product, category or customer.	search.gif
▣	Prints the current order on one page.	order_edit.gif

(icon)	Displays the relevant link to the product or category so you can integrate it with an existing site.	link.gif
(icon)	Takes you to the next list of items. (this is a yellow arrow)	next.gif
(icon)	Takes you to the previous list of items. (this is a yellow arrow)	prev.gif
(icon)	Allows you to move the product, category or other item down in the listing, which will be reflected at the actual online store.	move_d.gif
(icon)	Allows you to move the product, category or other item up in the listing, which will be reflected at the actual online store.	move_u.gif
(icon)	Refreshes the list.	refresh.gif
(icon)	Launches a page from Miva's site which will explain the option or function.	help.gif
LOGOUT	Logs users out of the admin area.	logout4x.gif
MAIN	Takes you back to the main screen.	main4x.gif
DOCS	Takes you to Miva documentation section on their site.	docs4x.gif
SUPPORT	Takes you to the support section of the Miva site.	support4x.gif
(icon)	Takes you to the Miva web site.	blades4x.gif

Key Help Features

Throughout the Admin area, there is a (icon) button in the upper right-hand corner. This will launch a new window with a brief description of the task at hand. While it may not provide detailed information, it will help remind you of the process to carry out a task.

Using Lists

Miva Merchant displays products, categories, customers and other information in lists. By default, 10 items are displayed per page, with next and previous buttons. This can get frustrating when you have hundreds of products or customers.

At any time, at the bottom of each list, you can enter a new pagination number and then click the refresh button to re-display the list.

File Extensions

When compiled Miva Merchant was released, the core script file format changed. The result is faster processing, among other things that are beyond the scope of this book.

Miva Merchant versions 4.14 and higher have a different file extension than prior versions. Previous versions carry a file extension of .mv, while compiled Miva Merchant (versions 4.14+) carry a file extension of .mvc. Since this book focuses on the latest versions available at the time of printing, references to .mvc are used.

If you are running uncompiled Miva Merchant (version 4.13 or lower), you will need to substitute .mv for .mvc when referenced throughout the book.

Chapter One

We know you're eager to just jump right in and get rolling with Miva Merchant. Problem is, there are some things you need to know before getting started—things that will lessen the frustration when it comes to standard tasks. Don't worry, we'll keep it short.

A Mall vs. A Store

Miva Merchant stores are housed inside of a "mall"* setting created by Miva Merchant upon setup. To the potential customer, this is simply a directory visitors hit on the first screen called by Miva Merchant, but *only* when there is more than one store. Otherwise, the single store is entered immediately.

Additional stores can be added to the mall by obtaining additional store licenses. This means you can have one, five, even twenty stores in your mall. Each store runs on its own, just like in an brick and mortar shopping mall. Each store runs independently—each has its own databases, search function and checkout.

When starting out you will only work with one store. Handling several stores in a mall will require some other duties as well and you really need to understand how Miva Merchant works before planning to maintain additional stores.

* Miva Corp now calls the "mall" a domain. To avoid confusion, we call it a mall.

Understanding Miva Files and Directories

This is the most difficult thing you will learn in this book. Not that it's absolutely necessary for a beginner to understand directory structures, but it does help in locating files if you need to make backups or obtain technical support.

> ✔ **We begin with the assumption that Miva Merchant is already installed on your server, and that the Setup script has already been run. If you obtained your license through a hosting company, this is most likely the case. If you obtained your copy of Miva Merchant directly from Miva Corporation or one of its non-hosting resellers, you may have to install it yourself. See Appendix A to learn how to install and setup Miva Merchant.**

Miva Merchant utilizes files from two different directories on the server. They are both named either Merchant or Merchant2, yet each is housed in a different parent directory on the server. The different parent directories generally referred to as script and data, but may have many different actual names:

✔ **By default, Miva Merchant versions 2.0 and higher were configured to install in the Merchant2 directory, so many hosting companies will continue to use this directory. However, some hosting companies install Miva Merchant in a directory named simply Merchant (no "2"), or may even use a different directory name (such as store or shop). For this reason, and to avoid confusion, we will always refer to the directory as /Merchant/.**

The Miva Merchant Script Folder

The /Merchant/ (or other directory) housed in the public directory of the server houses the script files that make Miva Merchant run properly. This directory is housed inside the servers public folder (usually named html, www or htdocs)—it is the same folder that contains your domain's index.html file.

The Miva Merchant script contains files and subdirectories of Miva Script files (the extension for this is .mvc— or .mv). It also houses a graphics folder, which contains images and buttons for your Miva Merchant Admin. By default, unless customizations are made, your store's product images (and any other images you upload via the Admin) will also be housed here.

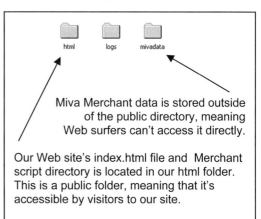

Images for your Miva Merchant store's product line are, by default, stored in the **../Merchant/graphics/0000000X** folder, where "X" denotes the store number. The first store you create will be labeled 00000001, and if another is added, its folder will be 00000002, and so on. (there are seven ZEROS and one digit for stores 1-9, and six zeros and two digits for 10-99, and so on).

Miva Merchant data is stored outside of the public directory, meaning Web surfers can't access it directly.

Our Web site's index.html file and Merchant script directory is located in our html folder. This is a public folder, meaning that it's accessible by visitors to our site.

✔ **If you add, delete a store, then add it again, a number will be skipped. Therefore, your current store might be numbered 00000003, and so on.**

Third-party modules are usually installed in the **/Merchant/4.xx/modules** directory, or a sub-directory thereof. However, unless the process calls for manually uploading a file, you should use the standard installation directions for installing modules.

2.x and 3.x users:

The path to this directory will instead be /Merchant/modules – the version-specific directory was not added until version 4.00.

The Miva Merchant Data Directory

The database files store all of Miva Merchant's data (for products, categories, orders, etc.) is housed outside the public directory inside a data folder. For some this folder is called **mivadata**, for others **htsdata**, or simply **data**. No matter what it's named, these "folders" do the same thing – contain important files for your online store. Database files, including information about products, customers and categories and orders are stored here. The store's data folder is to be stored in the root of your server (outside both the Merchant and regular HTML directories).

 Some installs by individuals or host providers will result in such files being placed directly in the Merchant (or relative) directory beneath the public HTML directory for your site. If this is the case, there may be a security issue. Data files need to be inaccessible to Internet users visiting your site.

Never, ever, ever open any of your store's data files unless you know exactly what you are doing. If we were to take a survey, results would probably show that 85% of new users who open these files without direction, and try to make changes, damage the files in one way or another. And the end results could be a totally corrupt store that won't operate unless everything is reinstalled, or you pay someone to fix it. Translation: you could make a $100+ mistake, and who's got money to burn?

If you're a new user, and you are not familiar with how these files work, don't touch them. Don't even touch the folder they reside in unless a technician instructs you to do so. Your initial goal is to setup a store, not crash it in the first week.

What Do I Need to Know? About Miva Script and HTML

Miva Merchant utilizes Miva Script. All third-party plug-ins, and some customizations, are written in Miva Script. This often scares new users of Miva Merchant, thinking they may need to learn Miva Script as a language. This is not the case. You need not understand any coding other than some elements of HTML, depending on the amount of customization you plan to make for your store.

Miva Merchant is a complete e-commerce package, including script and database files. However, all sites should start with an HTML home page, as the store does not load right from the domain address. If you know enough HTML to create your own home page, great! You're one step ahead of the game. If you do not understand how to create this page, you should either learn HTML (really learn it, not just throw something together) or you should contact a developer to create the page for you.

> *A brief tutorial on making the Miva Merchant Storefront your Web site's home page can be found in Chapter Ten: Existing Web Site Integration.*

If you are familiar with HTML, then you'll better understand how you can use this language within your store, such as with headers and footers, and other messages. We've included a brief list of common HTML tags in Appendix B to help you when needing to assign specific fonts or font attributes, such as bold and italic.

 Some hosts will configure your Web site so when a visitor types in your domain name it will automatically load the Miva Merchant storefront. Or, you could create an index home page file that does the same. The only drawback is that you may lose some key benefits with search engine placement.

Before You Delve... There are Two Ways...

We'll stay away from "wrong way" and "right way." Instead we look at the "long way" and "short way." Shortcuts are nice, but they can be useless when something doesn't happen the way you anticipated.

Let's say you just moved to a large city and you want to get from one end to the other. Obviously there are quick ways and not-so-quick ways. The long way is to take the most direct route—which probably takes you through all the rush-hour traffic. It's long, but it's the route you start with because you have no idea where you are.

After a few weeks, you become more comfortable and dare to step off that main route where there is less traffic, to shave a good 10 minutes off your daily trip. So you get a map, try the route on a weekend and get to know the neighborhoods. Soon enough you now can sleep until 7:30 a.m. when before you had to wake up at 6:45 a.m.

You can now take the "shortcut" because you know where you are. You also know more than one route, and can veer off to other streets if you need to.

Miva Merchant works the same way in many cases. **Wizards** were introduced in version 2.10. While they seem to take longer, they are considered shortcuts because they are more "foolproof." However, they don't really help you understand how Miva Merchant works. Wizards are perfect if you have a full-time administrator and only want to perform tasks yourself once in a while. But if you want to save money, and ultimately time, you need to understand all the elements of the Miva Merchant Admin.

Also, version 4.x release introduced a simple administration (for users who want to just put their store together and let it run), and an advanced administration (for those who really want to tweak it). Still, it's best to understand how the program works.

 We have noted throughout the tutorial those functions which can also be done with Wizards. Whenever you see this icon, it means the task can be done with a Wizard.

Wizards are covered at the END of this tutorial. And chances are, after you've gone step-by-step through this entire tutorial, you'll only glance at them once or twice. Wizards, though easier to use, actually take longer than doing something by advanced methods. They also don't give you as many options when setting up products and categories.

Most users who started with Wizards are shocked to find they can do things differently. Those who are later introduced to the advanced administration mode wind up staying there because it gives them more control.

Chapter Two

Preparing to Build the Store

We know you want to jump right in, but you can save some time (and probably money, too) by first sitting down and thinking about what you want your store to look like. Consider the layout that will look best for what you are selling. The most important issue to keep in mind is how your customers will react to your e-commerce site. It must be easy to navigate, pleasing to the eye, and must never, *ever*, make them feel like they are stupid because they can't find a product you carry. In short, you want to idiot-proof your store without making your customers feel like idiots.

By taking some early steps, you can avoid vast amounts of trial and error with your potential customers. It is up to you to make them one-time customers or repeat customers.

Start surfing the Internet. Bookmark sites you like, and take notes on why they work! They don't even have to be stores that carry a similar product line. In fact, look at the big guys, like **amazon.com** and **cooking.com**. See why they work! Then consider aspects of them for your own store. Note, however, that it is bad business to just copy someone else's design—it's a sure way to start off on the wrong foot, and it could lead to legal repercussions.

Do I need a design before I start? No, but having a mock layout that includes some initial content (such as a welcome message to your customer, store policies, etc.) will provide better insight on the direction your online store will take during its creation. At the very least, you *should* have a design in place on the live store before you open shop. Potential customers should not see your initial work in progress.

Store and Site Content

Your online store needs more than just products and categories. You also need content, including a sales pitch (a paragraph or two on the first page telling people who you are, what you offer and why they should shop with you). Your site also needs to list policies, such as shipping, privacy, guarantees, return information, etc. Now is the time to get this information together, as it will play a role in how you design the navigation for your Miva Merchant store.

Preparing the Products and Categories

Before creating your store, you should sit down and determine how you will number (**code**) your products. If you already have an inventory system, then you can use the codes (item numbers, skus, etc.) you already have (these should be only numbers and letters, dashes and underscores).

If you do not currently have a product coding method, take a few moments to consider the best logical method. Some stores create alphanumeric codes that help them identify products by the code alone. Others will just start at a number, such as 1001, and increment the number by one each time they add a product. Some store owners code products with the product name, substituting underscores (_) for spaces, for both quick identification and search engines.

 You cannot use spaces or other special characters for any codes. Miva Merchant will reject them. It could also affect future synching of data with other solutions.

You should also sketch out an outline showing which categories products will fall into. You will want to utilize the Miva Merchant categorization system to better list the items you will be selling.

And, yes! You can assign products to multiple categories in Miva Merchant. Cross reference as much as you wish—your potential customers will thank you for doing so!

Considering Navigation

You need a navigation that's simple, so grab a cup of java (or your favorite beverage) and study the notes you took while visiting other online stores. This will help you configure your store's navigation. If you want to implement your own creative design, work out a template either on paper or in a graphics program (like Adobe Photoshop) or HTML editor.

Keep in mind that potential customers must understand your navigation. Many times new store owners marry their ideas because they know how everything works. Be prepared to compromise—what you think is a cool feature or an evident shopping menu may not be for many visitors.

Think About Features

Chances are there are some features you'll want that Miva Merchant doesn't offer. Now is the time to write them down. You can later spend time locating solutions from either Miva Corp. or various Certified Business Partners.

Many new users of Miva Merchant are buy happy when it comes to add-ons and modules. They want to add features without considering what the needs really are. Consider your needs first, then seek out the solutions.

The Layout & Style

Miva Merchant calls the basic layout of the store the "look and feel," and with your store license you get a choice of two – the **Miva Merchant User Interface (MMUI)** and **KoolCat (KCUI)**.

While KoolCat is supported by current versions of Miva Merchant, the company hasn't made any updates or enhancements to the interface in years, and has no plans to. Also, many current third-party modules will not work with this user interface. In short, it's not a popular interface and most full-fledged stores that use it have been doing so since a version 1.x.

There is a third-party solution called the **Open Look and Feel** (OpenUI), which enhances Miva Merchant and makes it easier for third-party modules (like coupon and design modules) to simply plug in and work. The OpenUI has become a standard and Miva Corp. also supports the user interface. We'll discuss the OpenUI later, as it is worth your consideration.

Recently, Copernicus Business Systems created the **Dynamic Templates for MMUI** module, which instead allows Miva Merchant users to create template HTML files for all the design elements of Miva Merchant. Dynamic Templates also supports the installation of most third-party modules without requiring coding changes, and it can be used in conjunction with the OpenUI.

Colors and Fonts

Miva Merchant will let you specify which **colors** are used for the background of the category tree (the list of categories, normally appearing on the left side of the screen), the navigation bar (usually located at the top of each page) and other areas. It will also let you choose the **fonts** (typestyles) and font sizes and colors for various aspects of your store. Again, you need to choose what works best with your site.

> Whenever you see the ⬤ button, you can change the color settings for the item.

For example, if you only sell 100 products in three categories, you might choose a large font for your category links. However, if you have 20 categories, you might choose a smaller font. It all depends on what works best. You'll find in-depth information on fonts and their use on the WWW in **Appendix B**.

Images, Graphics, and More Graphics

There's no doubt why some Web sites just suck the visitors right in. A simple layout with killer graphics can be very effective. Page load time, however, is a huge issue. You can have the best graphics for a store of your type, but if it takes a full minute for the pages to load, many potential customers will leave.

> Whenever you see the ⬠ button, you can upload an image for the item.

When creating custom graphics and scanning images for your store, pay attention to file size and load time respectively. For information on image file types and their use on the WWW, including resolution and sizing, see **Appendix B**.

Payment Processing

Obviously you need to have a way to collect payment. Collecting only checks will put a damper on your sales—people are impulse buyers and many prefer the ease of using a credit card when purchasing products online. If you don't have a credit card merchant account, you will need to shop around for one.

There are two ways to process credit card orders with Miva Merchant. You can either receive the payment information and process it manually, or use a real-time payment gateway which validates funds before the order is actually submitted. Miva Merchant comes with modules for some merchant and authorization services, and you'll find information about them in **Appendix C**.

✔ **PayPal is a widely accepted, and expected, payment feature as well. Most online stores now accept this alternative means of paying with a credit card.**

How To Ship?

You need to decide how you will ship orders. You may decide to use UPS, USPS, FEDEX, Airborne, or other carriers. You may also sell products customers will download (incurring no shipping charges). Finding out up front the most effective shipping methods for you will not only make the configuration process easier, but it will give you the ability to charge accurate and competitive shipping costs.

✔ *Don't worry if your shipping methods are not included in Miva Merchant. Chances are there is a third-party module that has been or can be created for your store.*

Sales Tax

Chances are there are tax laws you must follow. Miva Merchant supports for shopper-selected and state-based sales tax for the US, and various VAT tax structures for foreign businesses. Consider which method you need to use. When you create your store you will need to tell Miva Merchant how to configure sales tax.

Additional Features

Most online stores consist of more than just products, categories and various shipping and payment options. You'll also want to consider how you will handle other aspects of the store, such as inventory, product options and customer accounts. Do you want to run an affiliate program? You can with Miva Merchant.

Some features (either design or functional aspects) may require third-party modules. Take time to think about them.

Don't just add a feature because another site has that feature. Make sure that whatever features you plan to use is relevant for your online store, your products and your customers. For example, a feature that lets potential customers rate products they already have is only useful if the product line warrants discussion and review, such as books, music and electronics items. There's a difference between rating a store's service and its products, so if you sell clothing, a feature to review your products probably isn't warranted.

When it comes to adding features, don't just start buying and/or installing anything you think is cool—doing so is probably a waste of at least some of your funds. Instead, decide on the features your Miva Merchant store needs, then seek out the solution.

Chapter Three

Working with the Admin

Anything you need to do to create your online store is performed in the Miva Merchant Administration Area. **We'll call it the Admin**.

Remember that we won't be covering any coding here, so essentially every step we take to manipulate how the store looks will be done in the Admin screens.

Logging Into the Admin

Depending on your hosting provider, and the way Miva Merchant was installed on the server, the web address to log into your store's admin area should resemble one of these URLs:

https://www.yoursite.com/Merchant/admin.mvc

https://www.yoursite.com/cgi-bin/miva?Merchant/admin.mvc

Remember: If you're running Miva Merchant version 4.13 or lower, the "c" will be dropped off the file extension.

Miva Merchant gives you two log in options: regular or secure (using SSL encryption). By logging in securely you take measures to further protect your store. However, you may have to make certain changes in the Admin before you can login securely.

To login securely, you need a secure URL, which may or may not include your actual domain name. Check with your host to find out what your secure URL to Miva Merchant will be.

If you do not yet have an SSL certificate for your domain, you can drop the "s" off the URL, and log in regularly. If you access your Admin's login screen in regular mode, and secure mode is available, you will see a link for logging in securely.

 Your online store needs SSL so information during the checkout and account procedures (customer information, credit card data, etc.) may be transmitted securely. Most merchant accounts require this, and many customers will leave stores that do not use SSL.

When you log into the Admin for the first time you are prompted with the Simple Administration Screen. This is the "beginners" screen that walks you through the basic tasks of setting up your store.

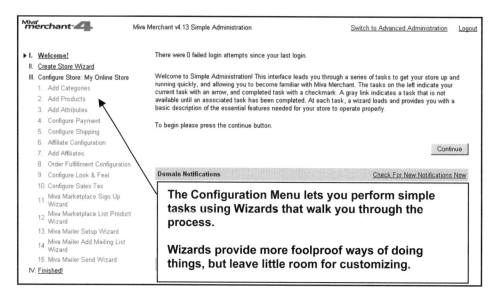

Based on the screen above, you see that you can use simple menu wizards to create categories, products, attributes, and so on. Even though Miva Merchant prompts you to start here, there are drawbacks.

For example, when adding products using Wizards, Miva Merchant builds a product code for you. Also, as we stated earlier, learning the short way really isn't as beneficial as learning the long way first.

So, we will skip this section for now. It is recommended that you follow this book as it is written in order to gain the best understanding on how Miva Merchant works.

Click the <u>Switch to Advanced Administration</u> link in the upper right-hand corner.

Advanced Administration

The Admin area consists of three core sections:

The Navigation Bar
Contains the Main (takes you back to the initial main screen), Docs (linked to documentation at miva.com), Support (at miva.com) and Log Out links.

The Admin Menu
The left-hand menu which contains links to all the core features you can use. The blue arrows to the left of text indicate a section or group. Clicking the arrow will result in additional options being listed below the main topic.

The Main Admin Area
This is the large area on the right. When you use the Admin Menu, to edit your store, Miva Merchant will display all information and forms for completing a task in this main screen.

When you first login to Miva Merchant, this screen will default to the "main" screen, which contains information about the Miva Merchant version you are running, simple statistics, notification messages and links for Wizards.

Miva Merchant has a timeout feature. If you don't utilize this area for a default of 60 minutes, it will automatically log you out. You could later extend this time if you wish, but safe is always better than sorry.

The Admin Navigation Structure

Miva Merchant's administrative area uses tier-level menus for various settings. Here's a breakdown of where you will find features that can be manipulated. They are explained in detail throughout the following chapters.

MALL SETTINGS

Mall Settings are settings that apply to the overall mall. Unless you use a different look and feel file (or .mvc file) for each store, all stores will follow the same standard formats. Some individual store settings can be different, and you'll learn about these later.

Refresh—reloads the Admin Menu to represent the last saved changes

Main—takes you back to the main screen you see when you first log in

Domain Settings—settings required for Miva Merchant to operate

> **Information**—the site's domain name, the Miva Merchant license number and the Miva Merchant version number
> **Registration**—the licensee's name and contact information
> **Site Configuration**—URLs and Secure URLs used for graphics and files
> **Timeouts**—how long a shopper can be idle before their incomplete order is dumped (default is 60 minutes)

Store Selection Layout—how your mall will look (initially displayed *only* when there is more than one store)

> **Layout**—available Look and Feel options
> **Display**—how the listing of stores in the mall is displayed
> **Colors**—background, link and navigation bar color settings
> **Fonts**—default font (if not specified elsewhere)
> **Images**—navigation bar logo, store selection logo (for your mall)

Users—you can add and assign permissions to various administrative users

Modules—modules that are available to be assigned to the store

Wizards—step-by-step screens for simply creating products, categories and implementing other basic features

Stores—by default there is one store, but more may be added. Many additional options will be available under this listing once the store is added.

Utilities—contains the "pack data" function for maintenance on all mall databases (a different packing utility is used for each individual store)

Switch to Simple Administration—takes you back to the simple Admin area where you can just use Wizards to build your store

About Miva Merchant—licensing and registration information

Logout—logs you out from the Admin area

Chapter Four

Setting Up the Store

How your store looks can play a big role in whether or not visitors become customers. Selecting the right layout, colors, fonts and graphics is vital.

Throughout the exercises in this book we'll direct you to use the ▶ (right arrow) to drop down menus in the Admin Menu. Sometimes, as you may have completed previous exercises, this will be replaced by the ▼ (down arrow). When this happens, you can skip the step as it has already been completed.

Remember:
Whenever we say Admin Menu we are referring to the menu of links and sub-menus on the left-hand side of the screen. When actual links are clicked on here, the screen on the right will load the content (input forms, etc.).

Before we start, we're going to take a look at the "default" settings for all stores. By this, we mean the settings all stores in this mall will have unless you make changes.

Assigning Default Store Settings

You are able to set **Store Settings** for each individual store. The mall includes defaults that will be used for each store before changes are made in the actual store's settings. Changes are not necessarily required here, and any changes that are made will affect all stores unless you create settings for each store individually (recommended).

Remember, we are the advanced administration mode.

STEP BY STEP

1. In the Admin Menu for the mall, click the **Store Selection Layout** link.

2. Select the **Miva Merchant Look & Feel** layout.

3. Click the **Display** link. By default, if you have only one store, the Miva Merchant URL (www.yourdomain.com/Merchant2/merchant.mvc) will go directly to that store. If you have more than one store, a Mall page will be displayed. Here, you can tell Miva Merchant how many store names to display per line, and if you want any information to be displayed above those links.

✔ *Some hosts mistakenly configure the server so Miva Merchant will not run unless the www is included as part of the URL. While you can work around this by making sure all links point to the full domain name, including the www., it's better to request the host fix the issue.*

4. Click the **Colors** link.

5. Use the 🔲 button to select colors from a grid. You can set default colors for:

Body Background
The background color of the entire store

Body Text
The font color for all standard text throughout the store

Body Link
The font color for all links throughout the store

Body Active Link
The font color of a link while the potential customer is being taken to the proper page

Store Selection Layout		
Layout Display **Colors** Fonts Images		
Body Background:	#ffffff	🔲
Body Text:		🔲
Body Link:		🔲
Body Active Link:		🔲
Body Viewed Link:		🔲
Navigation Bar Background:	#000000	🔲

Body Viewed Link
The font color of a link when the potential customer has already viewed the page

Navigation Bar Background
The background color of the bar at the top of the screen that contains the buttons Storefront, Basket, etc.

✔ *If you know the hexadecimal value for the color values (a combination of six numbers and/or letters), you can enter them in the input boxes.*

6. Click the **Fonts** link.

By default, the font for the store is **Arial** as a first choice, and **Helvetica** as a second. This means if a user does not have the Arial font installed on his or her own computer, the Helvetica font will be displayed instead (PC users normally use Arial, and MAC users normally use Helvetica). If the visitor has neither font installed, the browser's own default font (which could be anything) will be used.

Verdana is another popular font, as are Times (MAC) and Times New Roman (PC). Most other fonts should be avoided as they may not be installed on the user's computer, so they won't see the store as you do. For more information on Fonts, see *Appendix B*.

7. Click the **Images** link.

Store Selection Layout		
Layout Display Colors Fonts **Images**		
Body Background:		
Navigation Bar Logo:	graphics/en-US/mmui/blades.gif	
Navigation Bar "Select Store":	graphics/en-US/mmui/selstr.gif	

By default, Miva Merchant assigns its own images for Store Selection for malls (if the visitor is in one store, and wants to access another in a mall), and an image which will return him or her back to the index page of the actual Web Site (domain page) – this is the blades.gif image. You can also set a body background image here.

Let's not worry about these images right now – they can be changed later within the individual store.

 Remember, these and additional settings can be applied to individual stores, so if you plan to have more than one store, you might want to skip these altogether.

Adding the Main Store

Through most of this book, we refer to the mall as having just one store. You can have more than one store within your mall. While we will discuss the different settings for the store, we won't be delving into actual coding (the actual scripting language that makes Miva Merchant run) for different stores.

Most e-commerce sites will only run one store. Any additional stores you want to add (later, let's get through the basics first), will run on the same domain as the original.

Before you can create products and categories, you must first create your store.

STEP BY STEP

1. In the Admin Menu, click the ▶ next to **Stores**.

2. Click the **Add Store** link.

The administrative login created during the installation of Miva Merchant is automatically entered. By default, this is the main administrator for the store.

You can always create another login and make that the main administrator, but, for security reasons, we recommend you keep your initial login as the manager for the store, and then add more logins later, perhaps giving each specific permissions.

3. Enter a **store code** - a short code for the store (do not use special characters or spaces).

4. Enter a **name for the store** - this is the actual store name and can contain spaces and any characters you'd like. This is the name visitors to your store will see in the browser title bar.

When visitors navigate Web sites, the browser's title bar tells them where they are.

This title is also logged as the default name in their browser's bookmark or favorites directory.

5. Click the **Owner** link at the top. The licensee information entered during setup will already be filled in. If necessary, make any changes.

6. Click the **Settings** link at the top.

7. Enter the following:

The **Units of Measurement** you will use (pounds or ounces). The weight is used for shipping calculations and will also, by default, be displayed on the product screen.

The **Basket Timeout**—How many minutes a shopper can be idle before the basket "times out" and the customer will need to start over. We recommend leaving this at the default of 60 minutes.

The **Price Group Overlap Resolution**—We'll discuss this later, but basically, if you use Miva Merchant's feature to offer discounts to specific customers, you'll want to set this to use the lowest price.

The **First Order #**—Miva Merchant will automatically increment each order number by "1." The initial order number cannot later be changed without developer modifications.

Sales Tax Calculation - How sales tax will be configured; if no tax will be used, choose state-based.

Currency Formatting - Which currency your store will use.

8. Click the **Layout** link at the top.

We suggest you use initially the **Miva Merchant Look & Feel**. If you're dying to see what the KoolCat v1.x Look & Feel looks like and the Appendix at the back of this book isn't good enough, we suggest you choose it now, take a look, then switch. The OpenUI may also be an option. You may select this now, however, it will present additional menu options throughout the store which are not discussed in this book.

 Switching Look & Feels without export and import procedures (such as those supplied with the OpenUI) later will result in the loss of settings and you will be stuck having to redesign your store. You will also lose all Headers and Footers, among other customizations.

9. Click the **Add** button.

Store Settings

After adding your store, you will see additional features listed in the Admin Menu. You'll find these by clicking the ▶ next to your store's name.

Don't feel compelled to understand all these features right now; this is just a list of what you will be learning how to do in Miva Merchant.

- Refresh
- Main
- Shop Miva General Store
- Shop Miva Warehouse
- Domain Settings
- Store Selection Layout
- ▶ Users
- ▶ Modules
- ▶ Wizards
- ▼ Stores
  - Add Store
  - ▶ MvCommerce.Net TEST STORE
  - ▼ MvCommerce.Net
    - ▶ Wizards
    - ▶ Groups
    - Countries
    - States
    - ▶ Categories
    - ▶ Products
    - ▶ Marketing
    - ▶ Attribute Templates
    - ▶ Upsale
    - Inventory
    - ▶ Affiliate Configuration
    - Shipping Configuration
    - Payment Configuration
    - ▶ Order Fulfillment Configuration
    - Logging Configuration
    - ▶ System Extension Configuration
    - ▶ Customers
    - ▶ Availability Groups
    - ▶ Price Groups
    - ▶ Order Processing
    - ▶ Utilities
- ▶ Utilities
- Switch to Simple Administration
- About Miva Merchant
- Logout

Wizards—Foolproof, but often limited, ways of performing tasks.

Groups—Used to assign permissions to different Admin users.

Countries—Denotes what countries you will accept orders from (and ship to).

States—You can select which states are available for shipping and tax.

Categories—Used to "group" products into like sections.

Products—Used to add products to the store.

Attribute Templates—Allows you to use templates for product options. **4X**

Upsale—Allows you to offer last-minute specials upon checkout. Upsell items are similar to the teaser aisle in a grocery store.

Inventory—Allows you to set options for managing product inventories. **4X**

Affiliate Configuration—Allows you to run an affiliate program for your store. **4X**

Shipping Configuration—Used to set shipping methods and rates.

Payment Configuration—Used to configure payment methods, including credit cards (manual or real-time gateways), checks and PayPal.

Order Fulfillment—Includes configurations for merchant and customer order email confirmations.

Logging—Allows you to log activity in your store for later analysis.

System Extension Configuration—Used for optional user interface modules from third-party developers.

Customers—Displays contact information for all shoppers and customers who have created an account.

Availability Groups—Allows you to make specific products available to select customers.

Price Groups—Allows you to set specific discounted pricing for select customers.

Order Processing—Used to view, update and process orders.

Utilities—Allows you to import and export orders, products and other information, and perform maintenance on the store.

Reaching Your Online Store

Once you have added your initial Miva Merchant store, you can view it online. To view the front end of your store, open a new browser window (leaving the Admin Area open in its own window) and enter the following URL, depending upon your host's configuration of the server:

http://www.yourdomain.com/Merchant/merchant.mvc

http://www.yoursite.com/cgi-bin/miva?Merchant/merchant.mvc

} *Tinybubbas.com/ shop/merchant.mvc*

✔ *If your host provider has given the "Merchant" directory a different name, you will need to edit this link.*

As you work through Admin and create your store, you will want to view the store itself regularly. Keep in mind that when you make changes, you will have to refresh the browser window for the front end in order to see them.

☛ **If for some reason your installation failed and the files are corrupt, call your host's Miva Corp.'s technical support. If there was a problem in the install process, and the problem occurs this early, it may be easier to re-install Miva Merchant than to try to fix the problem.**

Editing the Store

You just created your store, so why would you edit it? The Edit Store feature allows you to set particular options that weren't available when simply adding the store.

 Right now we're just walking through the different edit features. If you make any actual changes during this walk-through, be sure to click the Update button at the bottom of the screen or the changes will be lost.

STEP BY STEP

---

1. Click the ▶ next to **Stores**.

2. Click your store's link.

3. In the right-hand side of the screen, click the **Messages** link and enter some basic information (you can always change it later).

Store Front Welcome:

Here you enter the information a visitor will see when first accessing the store. It will basically be an index page to the store, but will also include the category tree on the left and navigation bar on the top, created by Miva Merchant on the fly. This section can include HTML. Use this space to hype new and hot products, provide links to other information, such as contact pages and ordering information. Do what you like with it.

Edit Store: MvCommerce.Net				
License	Identification	Owner	Settings	Layout
Maintenance Mode	Order Minimums	Customer Fields	State Based Sales Tax	Messages
Pagination	Colors	Fonts	Images	Headers & Footers
Buttons	Page Sections	Product List Layout	Search Layout	Related Products Layout
Product Display Layout	Customer Accounts			

Store Front Welcome: [text box]

Order Completed Thank You: Thank you for your order. Please keep this invoice for you [text box]

Update   Delete   Reset

If you use HTML in the welcome message (or anywhere else for that matter), <u>do not</u> include the <HTML>, <BODY> and <HEAD> tags. Miva Merchant pages are parsed as complete HTML coded source pages, so all standard tags will already be included in the source code for the screen. You may choose to use TABLES, but do not give the tables exact sizes (only one of the table's columns if need be), unless your design calls for it, as Miva Merchant will size the screens automatically to fit the browser window.

For information on screen sizes, resolution and other important information on creating these pages, see Appendix B.

Order Completed Thank You
This message is displayed at the top of the customer's final order page, also called the Invoice screen. Enter any information you want to be shown on the completed order page. For example:

> **Thank you for shopping STORE NAME. We appreciate your business. An email is en-route to you confirming this order, but please write your order number down should any problems occur. If you have further questions, please email <<EMAIL ADDRESS>> or call <<PHONE NUMBER>>.**

4. Click the **Pagination** link.

Product List:	○ Do Not Paginate		
	⊙ Display 20	Products per page	
Search Results:	○ Do Not Paginate		
	⊙ Display 20	Products per page	

You can tell Miva Merchant how many products to list per page on both the Search Results page and the Product List page. By default, there is no pagination, but if you have hundreds of products, or more, this can leave visitors waiting a long time for all the listings to load, and they'll have to scroll quite a bit.

We recommend setting this to no more than 20 items per page. **Next** and **Previous** buttons will be displayed at the bottom of each page of listings, and customers won't have to scroll extensively.

5. Click the **Customer Accounts** link.

Customers can create a login and Miva Merchant will then store the billing and shipping contact information (no payment info). Such accounts are required if you plan to offer discounts or product availability to select customers. This is discussed in more detail later.

Display Link Above Categories – this optional feature will display a "Customer Login" link above the listing of categories in your store. If a customer already has created a customer account, it can display a salutation, and his or her name. Otherwise, it will display a prompt for either "Existing Customers" or a sign-in prompt which you will name.

Customer Login Link – you can signify the text shoppers will read, prompting them to either login or create an account.

Customer Account Link – you can select the greeting for logged in customers, such as "hello, NAME". You can have Miva Merchant display the first name, the first and last names, or no names. You can also add additional text. Keep it short.

	☑ Display Links Above Categories			
Customer Login Link:	Existing Customers			
Customer Account Link:	Hi,	○ None ○ First Name ⊙ First Name Last Name	!	
	☑ Display Login Before Order Form			

In our example we put "Hi," in the first box, selected First Name and then entered "!" in the second box. This will display to the customer as: Hi, Tina! or Hi, Sam!

Display Login Before Order Form – when a customer decides to checkout, you can alert them to either login, create a customer account, or to checkout without creating an account. If you do not use this feature, then the customer will be prompted to enter shipping and billing information, but will not be prompted to create an account or login to an existing account.

> ***Should I use Customer Accounts?***
> If you expect customers to order frequently, or if you plan to offer special pricing or exclusive products to select customers, you'll want to use Customer Accounts. Some third-party modules, such as ones that allow customers to view their orders history (print prior invoices) or reorder based off a prior order, require that Customer Accounts be used.
>
> Customer Accounts are also useful if you plan to use email marketing (such as Miva Mailer) as part of your marketing strategies.
>
> If your customers will likely only order once, and you have no real needs for maintaining this information, you may not want to implement Customer Accounts. You will always receive the customer's information with the actual order.

6. Click the **Colors** link.

   You can select the color theme for your store on various aspects. See the next page for a table outlining which items can have assigned colors.

To change any of the colors, just click the Select Color button next to each item, or enter the hex-color value in the text box.

Color Item	What it Affects
Body Background	The background color of each page. We recommend using either white or black.
Body Text	The color of standard text. We recommend either white or black.
Body Link	The color of any linked text.
Body Active Link	The color a link changes to while the link is being activated.
Body Viewed Link	The color of a link after it has been clicked; denotes the visitor has already visited that page or item.
Category Tree Background	The background color of the left menu which houses the category links. This can remain the same as background color, or you can assign another color to spice up the page.
Header Foreground	The color of the header text displayed in Category pages, such as the category title.
List Header Foreground	The color of the header on a product list page.
List Header Background	The background of the individual product lines on a product list page.
List Alternate Background	The alternate background (like shading every other line in a spreadsheet) of individual product lines on a product list page.
Navigation Bar Background	The background color of the Navigation Bar at the top of each page.

You'll find information on hex –color values in Appendix B.

7. Click the **Font**s link.

You can signify which fonts are used throughout the store. We recommend that you use only the five most common fonts found on computer systems, and no size smaller than −1. You should also assign more than one font, so if a customer does not have the first choice installed on his or her computer, the second choice will be displayed.

Body Text:	Face:	Arial, Helvetica, sans-serif
	Size:	2
Category Tree Text:	Face:	Arial, Helvetica, sans-serif
	Size:	1
Header Text:	Face:	Arial, Helvetica, sans-serif
	Size:	3
List Header Text:	Face:	Arial, Helvetica, sans-serif
	Size:	2

Serif Fonts
Serif fonts have little "hooks" on each letter.

<u>The font this sentence is typed in is a serif font – Times New Roman.</u> It is a default font on most machines.

When assigning this font, you should use: Times, Times New Roman – MAC users generally use Times, and PC users generally use the latter.

Sans Serif Fonts
Sans Serif fonts don't have "hooks."

<u>This sentence is typed in a sans serif font – Arial.</u>

When assigning this font, you should use: Arial, Helvetica, sans-serif – MAC users generally use Helvetica, and PC users generally use Arial. Sans-serif is another standard font.

Verdana and Tahoma are popular newer fonts, and are common with all newer PCs.

<u>This sentence is typed in Verdana.</u>
<u>This sentence is typed in Tahoma.</u>

To signify Verdana as the default font, enter Verdana, Tahoma, Arial, Helvetica. This way, if a computer does not have the Verdana nor Tahoma fonts installed, a sans-serif font is still displayed. Verdana will be the first choice.

If you assign any font the user does not have, the default font they've set in their browser will be used.

For more information on fonts and which font sizes you should use, see Appendix B.

8. Click the **Images** link.

Body Background:	[ ]
Navigation Bar Logo:	graphics/en-US/mmui/blades.gif
Navigation Bar Logo Link:	http://www.mvcommerce.net
Navigation Bar "Select Store":	graphics/en-US/mmui/selstr.gif
Navigation Bar "Store Front":	graphics/en-US/mmui/storfmt.gif
Navigation Bar "Account":	graphics/en-US/mmui/account.gif
Navigation Bar "Search":	graphics/en-US/mmui/search.gif
Navigation Bar "Product List":	graphics/en-US/mmui/prodlist.gif
Navigation Bar "Basket Contents":	graphics/en-US/mmui/basket.gif
Navigation Bar "Checkout":	graphics/en-US/mmui/checkout.gif

Miva Merchant includes a set of images (buttons) for store navigation. These include buttons shoppers can click on for the **Store Front, Basket Contents, Account, Checkout, Product List** and **Search**. You can opt to keep these buttons, however, your store will then look like many other Miva Merchant stores. "Out of the box" works, but it doesn't make you stand out.

Chances are you will want to change these standard graphics. For right now, however, leave these as they are. After learning to create your own buttons (**Appendix B**), and the uploading procedure, these changes can be made. We'll discuss these and other changes in *Chapter Ten: Fleshing Out the Store.*

You may opt, at this time, to enter the URL to your home page (index.html or index.htm for your site) in the **Navigation Bar Logo Link** box. It should be entered in one of the following formats:

http://www.yourdomain.com/index.html
../index.html

Or, you might want the logo link to go right to your Miva Merchant storefront. In that case, the link will resemble:

http://www.yourdomain.com/Merchant/merchant.mvc
Or, relatively: merchant.mvc?Screen=SFNT

The link you enter may be determined by how SSL is configured by the server. More information on this is discussed in a bit.

As you can see, there are many more options in the Edit Store section. We'll be getting into all of them as we work on the store, when we're ready to get beyond the basics.

Order Confirmation Messages

It is expected (as a standard) that when a customer places an order at your store, he/she will receive an email as well. This is called an order confirmation email.

You, as the merchant, may also want to receive an email whenever an order is placed.

Before editing the email notification systems, you first have to tell Miva Merchant you will use these methods for order processing.

STEP BY STEP

1. In the Admin Menu, click the ▶ next to stores, then the ▶ next to your store's link.

2. Click the **Order Fulfillment Configuration** link.

3. Put a check in the boxes next to both Customer Order Confirmation Email and Email Merchant Notification.

4. Click the **Update** button.

 Users of the OpenUI will have different modules to handle email notifications. If you are using the OpenUI, then checking off these particular options will result in two notification emails being sent for each order.

Email Merchant Notification

This feature will tell Miva Merchant to send an e-mail to you each time a customer places an order. The email will include the customer's shipping and billing contact information, the item(s) the customer ordered (including any attributes or options), any tax applied, and a the grant total. It will not include payment information – you will need to log into the admin area to retrieve this (see *Chapter Seven: Order Processing*).

 Email is not foolproof. A variety of things can happen that may result in you not receiving the email. Never rely on email notifications as the sole means of fulfilling orders.

STEP BY STEP

1. In the Admin Menu, click the **Order Fulfillment Configuration** link.

2. In the Order Fulfillment screen, click the **Email Merchant Notification** link.

| Modules | Customer Order Confirmation Email | Email Merchant Notification |

From: ○ Customer's Email Address
           ● Other: author@mvcommerce.net

To: author@mvcommerce.net

CC:

Subject: MvCommerce.net Order

Header (Precedes Order Information): The following order was placed:

3. Choose which **email address** you would like the order information to be **sent from**. This is usually set at the Customer's Email Address, but you can opt to have the return address be from another address.

 Some hosts will only allow this email to be sent from an address located at your domain.

4. Enter the email address the order information is to be **sent to**. This is usually the email address of the person responsible for processing orders.

5. If applicable, enter any other email address that should also receive the order information.

6. Enter the **Subject** of the message. Customers will not see this, as the email will be sent to the merchant.

7. Enter any prefix message to the order email in **header area**. You can change the words "Miva Merchant" to the store name. Again, customers will not see this.

8. Click the **Update** button.

Customer Order Confirmation Email

Most merchants will want to send immediate order confirmation to the customer; customers have come to expect this. Without utilizing this feature, chances are customers will email the merchant, asking if the order was ever received.

STEP BY STEP

1. In the Admin Menu, click the **Order Fulfillment Configuration** link.

2. In the Order Fulfillment screen, click the **Customer Order Confirmation Email** link.

| Modules | **Customer Order Confirmation Email** | Email Merchant Notification |

From: author@mvcommerce.net

CC:

Subject: Your MvCommerce.Net Order

Header (Precedes Order Information): Thank you for ordering with MvCommerc.net. Below are the details of your order. Orders placed by 3 p.m. EST are shipped the same day. Orders placed after this time are shipped on the following business day.

Should you have any questions, please contact us at: xxxxx@xxxxx.com or call us at (212)-555-5309.

3. In the **From** box, you should put the merchant's email address. This is the email address you want customers to reply to if they have questions.

4. If you want to send a copy of the email to other addresses, enter that address in the **CC:** box.

5. Enter the **Subject** of the message; it should be simple and should note that it is an order confirmation.

6. Enter the **Header** of the message; this is any information that precedes the confirmation of the customer's contact and ordering information. It should include the store name, estimated delivery time and contact information for the store (email and phone for customer queries).

   Miva Merchant will automatically "plug" the customer's billing and shipping contact information and order details.

    Do not use HTML for this message. If you want to send email confirmations in HTML, you'll need a third-party module. Note, however, that order confirmations should be in plain text as to avoid the problems of them getting filtered as SPAM.

7. Click the **Update** button.

Calculating Shipping Charges

Miva Merchant comes pre-installed with 8 or 9 shipping modules (depending on your version). They are:

Weight Table Based Shipping
Shipping based on a charge for a set weight range. Includes a handling charge. Also allows you to add additional shipping costs on a per product basis.

Price Table Based Shipping
Shipping based on the total order amount. Includes a handling charge.

Quantity Based Shipping
Shipping based on the number of items ordered.

Minimum Weight Shipping
Shipping based on an amount per unit (pound or ounce), with a minimum charge.

Flat Rate Shipping
A set amount per order.

Base + Weight Shipping
Shipping configured by a base fee plus an amount per item. **4x**

FedEx (versions 4.14+ Only)
Synchs with the FedEx gateway for real-time configurations.

U.S.P.S. Online Rate Calculation (versions 4.14+ Only)
Calculates both domestic and international shipping using the USPS gateway.

UPS Online (versions 4.0 – 4.13 Only)
Offers UPS rate calculations.

    All standard shipping modules that do not use gateways with carriers are set to work with all customers, regardless of the ship-to location. If you need configure shipping manually, but need to charge different rates by country or state, you will need to seek out a third-party solution.

Assigning a Shipping Module

You can add and delete shipping modules as you need. However, if any orders have been placed using an active shipping configuration, those orders will need to be removed from the system before you can remove the shipping method OR the shipping module itself will need to be deactivated. This is discussed later.

Since you're just starting, feel free to add several shipping methods so you can decide which ones will work best for you. You can use more than one shipping method—customers will see available options. Most online stores should offer methods by at least two different carriers.

STEP BY STEP

1. In the Admin Menu, click the **Shipping Configuration** link.

2. For now, check off just one method you plan to use or want to consider. You can always add and/or remove more methods later.

☐	U.S.P.S. Online Rate Calculation (Domestic & International)
☐	FedEx(R) Shipping Cost Estimate
☐	Weight Table Based Shipping
☐	Price Table Based Shipping
☐	UPS Domestic Shipping Calculator
☐	Quantity Based Shipping
☐	Minimum or Weight Shipping
☐	Flat Rate Shipping
☐	Base + Weight Shipping

3. Click the **Update** button.

Next, we'll learn how to configure each shipping module that is included with Miva Merchant.

Weight Table Based Shipping

This module allows you to configure shipping based on the weight of the entire order. It also allows you to add a base handling charge to each order.

STEP BY STEP

1. After assigning this module, click on the **Weight Table Based Shipping** link at the top of the screen.

2. Click the ⬚ button in the top right corner of the configuration box.

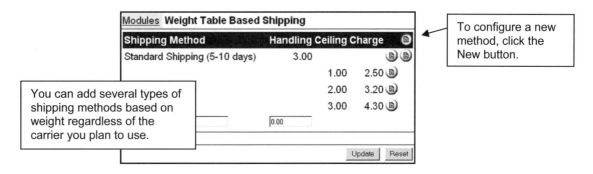

To configure a new method, click the New button.

You can add several types of shipping methods based on weight regardless of the carrier you plan to use.

3. Enter a name for this shipping method, such as "Standard Shipping." Your customers will see this label as a method selection during checkout.

4. In the **Handling** box, enter a base handling charge (can be 0.00). This amount will be applied once to each entire order, regardless of the total amount of the order.

5. Click the **Update** button. New empty fields will appear for this shipping method.

6. In the **Ceiling** box, enter the maximum weight of the order for which you will be charging a set price. In our example, this is 1 pound.

7. In the **Charge** box, enter the shipping charge for the ceiling weight you just entered. In our example this is 2.50. Do not include the $.

    ✔ *In our example here, if the total weight of the order is one pound, the customer will pay $3 handling, plus $2.50, making the total ship charge $5.50. If the total weight of the order is two pounds, the total ship charge will be $6.20.*

8. Click the **Update** button.

9. Continue steps 6 - 8 until all configurations are made for this shipping method.

10. To create a new method, such as "Priority Mail," click the ⬚ button at the top right again and repeat 3 - 9. Otherwise, you can move on to another task.

If you make a mistake on any method, you can…

Price Table Based Shipping

This module allows you to set shipping charges based on the total dollar amount of an order. You can also include a handling charge.

STEP BY STEP   **W**

---

1. After assigning this shipping method, click **the Price Table Based Shipping** link at the top of the screen.

2. Click the ⬜ button in the top right corner of the configuration box.

3. Enter a name for this shipping method, such as "Standard Shipping" or "USPS." Your customers will see this label as a method selection during checkout.

4. In the **Handling** box enter a base handling charge (it can be 0.00). This amount will be applied once to each and every order, regardless of the total amount of the order.

Shipping Configuration				
Modules **Price Table Based Shipping** Flat Rate Shipping				
Shipping Method	**Handling**	**Ceiling**	**Charge**	**%**
USPS	1.00			
		20.00	3.55	
		50.00	5.00	
		1000.00	10.00 %	
USPS Express Mail	5.00			
		0.00	0.00	
Shipping Configuration updated			Update	Reset

5. Click the **Update** button. New empty fields will appear for this shipping method.

6. Enter the ceiling and charges for each subtotal amount.

   In the **Ceiling** box, enter the maximum total of the order for which you will be charging a set price. In our example, this is 20.00. Do not include the $.

   In the **Charge** box, enter the shipping charge for the ceiling total you just entered. In our example this is 3.55. Do not include the $.

   If available in your version of Miva Merchant, you can also make the charge a percentage.

7. Click the **Update** button.

8. Continue steps 6 - 8 until all configurations are made for this shipping method.

9. To create a new method, such as "Express Mail," click the ⬜ button at the top right again and repeat 3 - 8.

In our example image above, if the order subtotal is $0.01 to $20.00, the customer will be charged $3.55 for shipping. If the subtotal of the order is $20.01 to $50.00, $5.00 shipping will be charged. If the subtotal of the order is more than $50.00 yet less than $1,000.00, the customer will be charged 10% of the order's subtotal for shipping.

Quantity Based Shipping

This module allows you to charge shipping by the quantity of products purchased. For example, you can charge one amount for 1-3 products; another amount for 4-5 products and a different amount for 6+ products. You can also charge a simple standard rate per product.

STEP BY STEP   **W**

1. After assigning this module, click the **Quantity Based Shipping** link at the top of the screen.

2. Click the button to add a method.

3. Enter the **Shipping Method**. Your customers will see this in the shipping selection pull-down menu during checkout.

4. If you will charge a total ship cost based on groups of quantities, check the **Prog** box (stands for **Progressive**). If you are charging per item based on how many items, leave this unchecked (for **Standard**).

5. Click the **Update** button.

6. Enter the floor and ceiling levels, and ship costs as shown in the following examples.

7. Click **Update** to complete your additions/changes.

There are two ways to configure the actual charges using the Quantity Based Shipping method. They are **Standard** and **Progressive**.

STANDARD (per item charge)

In the **Floor** box, enter the minimum number of items amount.

In the **Ceiling** box, enter the maximum number of items amount.

In the **Amount** box, enter the cost PER ITEM. Do not include the $ symbol.

For example, if you charge $2.00 per item for the first 3 items, $1 for 6-10 items, and $0.75 per item thereafter, you will have three calculations, shown here:

Remove	Shipping Method	Prog.	Floor	Ceiling	Amount/Unit
☐	Priority Mail				
☐			1	3	2.00
☐			4	10	1.00
☐			11	+	0.75

Use the plus sign (+) to denote an unlimited number of items.

If we want to add another method of shipping, such as overnight shipping, then we would click the button and name it Express, then enter our floors and ceilings for that method.

PROGRESSIVE (flat charge for range of items)

In the **Floor** box, enter the minimum number of items amount.

In the **Ceiling** box, enter the maximum number of items amount.

In the **Amount** box, enter the total ship cost. Do not include the $ symbol.

For example, if you charge $5 for 1-3 items, and $7 for 4-10 items, and $8 for 11+ items, you will have two calculations as shown here:

Remove Shipping Method	Prog.	Floor	Ceiling	Amount/Unit
☐ USPS Standard Mail	✓			
☐		1	3	5.00
☐		4	10	7.00
☐		11	+	8.00

Use the plus sign (+) to denote an unlimited number of items.

If we want to add another method of shipping, such as overnight shipping, then we would click the button and name it Express, then enter our floors and ceilings for that method.

Minimum or Weight Shipping

This module allows you to charge shipping by weight, but with a set minimum shipping amount no matter what is purchased. For example, if you charge $3.00 a pound, with a minimum ship charge of $5 (even if it's just 2 oz.), you will use this method.

With this method, you decide which shipping service to use. You also manually figure the ship cost per weight.

STEP BY STEP

1. After assigning this module, click the **Minimum or Weight Shipping** link at the top of the screen.

2. Click the ⒟ button to add a method.

3. Enter the **Shipping Method**. Your customers will see this in the shipping selection pull-down menu during checkout.

4. Enter the Amount/Weight Unit charge, which is the amount you will charge per each weight unit your store uses. For example, if you set Miva Merchant to handle weight in pounds, then this would be the charge per pound.

5. Enter the **Minimum Charge** amount—this is minimum ship charge that will be applied regardless of the weight of the order.

6. Repeat steps 2 – 5 for additional selections; each of these will be available in a shipping pull-down menu for the customer to select from.

7. Click the **Update** button.

Shipping Method	Amount/Weight Unit	Minimum Charge
FedEx Ground	1.25	5.00
USPS Priority Mail	1.50	3.85
	0.00	0.00

In this example, customers selecting USPS Priority Mail will be charged $1.50 per pound. However, the minimum charge is $3.85. Thus, even if the order is just one pound, the customer will be charged $3.85. Two pounds will also be $3.85 for shipping, but three pounds will run $4.50.

Flat Rate Shipping

The module allows you to charge a flat shipping rate regardless of the weight or subtotal of the order.

This module is useful if you want to offer free standard shipping. Since you can use more than one shipping module and method, you could use other configurations to allow customers to upgrade to a paid shipping option.

| STEP BY STEP | W |

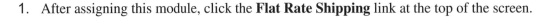

1. After assigning this module, click the **Flat Rate Shipping** link at the top of the screen.

2. Click the ⓓ button to add a method.

3. Enter the **Shipping Method**. Your customers will see this in the shipping selection pull-down menu during checkout.

4. In the **Amount** box, enter the flat rate the customer will be charged if selecting this shipping method.

5. Repeat steps 2 – 4 for any additional methods using Flat Rate Shipping.

6. Click the **Update** button.

Shipping Configuration	📷
Modules Flat Rate Shipping	
Remove Shipping Method	**Amount** ⓑ
☐ Standard Shipping - 5-10 days	5.95 ⓑ
Shipping Configuration updated	Update Reset

✔ *If you plan to use this module to offer a free standard shipping option, keep in mind that the option will be available to all customers, even if they are located in another country. If you need to restrict this type of shipping to a specific country, you'll need a third-party module.*

Base + Weight Shipping

This module allows you to charge a base shipping charge plus actual shipping charges based on the weight of the products ordered.

| STEP BY STEP | *W* |

1. After assigning this module, click the **Base + Weight Shipping** link at the top of the screen.

2. Click the ⊚ button to create a method.

3. Enter the **Shipping Method**. Your customers will see this in the shipping selection pull-down menu during checkout.

4. Enter the **Base Charge**, which is a handling charge that will be applied to each order.

5. In the **Amount/Weight Unit** box, enter the amount you will charge for each weight unit (such as pounds or ounces, as you setup in your store's settings).

<table>
<tr><td colspan="4">Shipping Configuration ⓘ</td><td>In this example, if a customer selects USPS Priority Mail, the shipping charge will be $4.95 PLUS $1.00 per pound. If the total weight of an order is three pounds, the shipping charge will be $7.95.</td></tr>
<tr><td colspan="4">Modules **Base + Weight Shipping** Flat Rate Shipping</td><td></td></tr>
<tr><td>Remove</td><td>Shipping Method</td><td>Base Charge</td><td>Amount/Weight Unit ⊚</td><td></td></tr>
<tr><td>☐</td><td>Standard Shipping</td><td>3.00</td><td>1.00 📖</td><td></td></tr>
<tr><td>☐</td><td>USPS Priority Mail</td><td>4.95</td><td>1.00 📖</td><td></td></tr>
<tr><td colspan="4">Update Reset</td><td></td></tr>
</table>

6. Repeat steps 2 – 5 as needed for additional methods.

7. Click the **Update** button.

UPS Domestic Shipping Calculator

This module works with rates provided by United Parcel Service.

Some versions of Miva Merchant do not include this module, and some versions have different configurable options.

| STEP BY STEP | |

1. After adding this module, click the **UPS** link at the top of the screen.

2. Complete the process by entering your UPS Registration Number, selecting your Rate Chart, adding any handling fee and selecting the services you want to offer to your customers.

3. Click the **Update** button.

FedEx

4XC

This module works with the FedEx gateway to configure shipping costs in real time. It requires that you already have a FedEx account (if you do not, visit **www.fedex.com**). This module requires OpenSSL on the server, which your host should have already installed. If not, you'll need to contact your host first.

| **STEP BY STEP** | **W** |

1. After assigning this module, click the **FedEx** link at the top of the screen.

2. For testing, select the **Default Test** option. To go live, select the **Default Production** option.

3. Enter your **FedEx Account Number**.

4. If you have a **Meter Number**, enter it here. If not, Miva Merchant will generate one for you.

5. Enter any handling charges.

    > **Base Handling Charge** – a flat fee charged to each order

    > **Additional Percentage Handling Charge** – a charge which represents a certain percent of each order

    > **Minimum Handling Charge** – the minimum shipping amount that must be applied to each order

6. Select your **Drop Off Type**.

7. If you want to require a signature for **Home Delivery** services, then check off the box.

8. Check off all services you will offer to your customers.

9. Click the **Update** button.

U.S.P.S. Online Rate Calculation

This module offers real-time calculations when shipping via the USPS. Usage requires that you first register at **www.uspswebtools.com**.

| **STEP BY STEP** | **W** |

1. After assigning this module, click the **U.S.P.S. Online Rate Calculation** link at the top of the screen.

2. Enter your assigned **USPS User ID** and **Password**.

3. Enter the **Source Zip code** (where the orders are shipped from).

4. Enter any **Handling** charge you want applied to each individual order.

5. Select the methods you want to offer to your customers.

6. Click the **Update** button.

Payment Configuration

In order to sell online you need to be able to take money. Okay, you knew this... While accepting checks is a good start, credit card acceptance is what will make or break your store.

There are things to consider when getting ready to launch an online store that accepts credit cards, and your decision will affect which settings are made in the Payment Configuration area.

A **merchant account** allows you to accept credit cards. A third-party **payment gateway** allows your store to approve credit card payments in real time. The gateway works with your merchant account, and it incurs its own separate fees.

You need to determine if you want to manually approve credit card payments (less expense, but takes more time) or if you want someone else to do this for you (more expensive, but takes less time). Basically, you need to determine what your time is worth, and which solution is the best for you and your customers.

Manual Processing vs. Gateway Processing

If you're expecting fewer than 10 orders per week, manually processing payments will probably be fine. Whether you will obtain a dial up merchant account, software enabled or one that requires a machine, each transaction will take you 2-3 minutes to process and log. This does not include the time needed for cross-referencing transactions to orders, etc. Overall, we've found that stores processing 20-30 orders per week will likely waste about 6-10 hours per month processing.

 There are also additional steps to take when processing credit cards manually outside of Miva Merchant. Since most merchant banks don't allow you to store the credit card information on the server, you would need to remove customer orders from Miva Merchant as you process them. You also can't work with the CVV2 or CID fields (those 3 and 4 digits on the front or back of the card used for further security, because these numbers are supposed to be passed encrypted.

A payment gateway will handle the processing for you, and many also give you access to a secure Web site to handle manual transactions (phone orders, etc.), run reports, credit and void sales and inquire about funds. Overall, we've found that stores processing 20-30 orders per week will spend less than 1 hour per month processing.

Another great benefit of using a gateway is not having to filter out bad orders. Any order that is successful after being run through a gateway is usually a good order. With manual processing, you have to check the cards, and notify customers after they've placed an order if there is a payment problem. This could result in a loss of sales.

The PayPal Advantage

With PayPal your customers can technically pay you with a credit card. However, using only PayPal will restrict your sales. While some customers prefer to pay via PayPal, this payment method will only account for a percentage of your sales.

We do, however, recommend that just about any online store accept PayPal, as it even allows people without credit cards to make online purchases that can be shipped quickly, either linked from a bank account or by using direct PayPal funds.

Assigning Payment Methods

Miva Merchant includes several payment acceptance options, and most premiere gateways are supported.

You must first set a payment options in order to accept any orders in the store. If you're just starting and don't yet have a merchant account (get one now, they can take several days), you can setup for check acceptance so you can test your store.

STEP BY STEP

1. In the Admin menu, click the **Payment Configuration** link.

2. Check off the payment types you will be using/accepting.

   If you will manually process credit card payments, select **Credit Card Payment With Simple Validation**.

   If you accept checks (not online checks, but paper checks in the mail), check the **Check Payment** option.

   To accept PayPal, check off the **PayPal Instant Notification** option.

3. Click the **Update** button.

If you selected any third-party payment gateway, then see Appendix C for additional information.

Credit Card Payment with Simple Validation

The **Simple Validation** method only verifies the card number the customer enters starts with the correct digit and contains the correct number of digits; it does not authorize funds or validate ownership. If you use this method, you will have to also click on the **Credit Card Payment With Simple Validation** link to deselect which card types you do not accept.

There are disadvantages to using this method. While it is less expensive (since it is not a gateway module, there are no additional fees on top of your merchant account), this feature does not allow for the collection of the CVV2 or CID fields (the three- or four-digit numbers on the front or back of the credit card). Many Internet-enabled merchant accounts are now requiring the collection of this information.

STEP BY STEP   **W**

---

1. After assigning this module, check off the **Credit Card Payment with Simple Validation** link at the top of the screen.

2. Uncheck any credit card types you will NOT accept.

3. Click the **Update** button.

 If you have issued store credit cards or need to re-implement a card, simply click the *button in the top right corner, and enter the appropriate data.*

COD Acceptance

You can allow customers to have items shipped to them **Cash On Delivery**. This method means you will ship the product and the customer will pay cash to the carrier upon delivery. This is not a fool-proof method; if the customer is not home, or refuses the package, you are stuck paying fees. However, you can impose those fees at the time of ordering.

Before accepting COD, check with your carrier and see what it charges for this type of delivery.

STEP BY STEP   **W**

---

1. After assigning this module, click the **COD** link at the top of the screen.

2. Enter the **Handling Charge** for COD payment.

3. Include any additional **message** for the customer choosing this method.

4. Click the **Update** button.

Check Payment

With this module, you only have the customer select to mail you a check, and enter the check number he or she will be sending. It does not offer verification services, nor does it collect data for Internet Checks.

When offering this payment method, be prepared to hold goods while the check is en route. Also be prepared to have to put goods back in stock as some people will not follow through.

STEP BY STEP	

    1. In Admin Menu, click on the **Payment Configuration** link.

    2. Check off Check Payment.

    3. Click **Update**.

PayPal Instant Payment Notification

This module works with PayPal itself to pass order totals to the PayPal gateway, and return the customer to your store's invoice screen once payment is complete.

Not all PayPal payments provide instant funds. Always check PayPal before shipping orders, as some people pay via check or other means that may have a hold time.

 The PayPal module included with Miva Merchant is a simple solution. If you need more robust features, such as subscription billing, etc., consider a third-party solution.

STEP BY STEP	

    1. After assigning this module, click the **PayPal Instant Payment Notification** link at the top of the screen.

    2. Enter your PayPal **Business Email** address.

    3. Select your **Currency**.

    4. Enter any **Message** for the customer to see when using this payment method.

    5. Click the **Update** button.

Viewing, Modifying & Deleting States

For US merchants, Miva Merchant includes a list of all states, and an option for Outside US. This list appears as a pull-down menu to the customer. It is also used for setting sales tax. You can modify this list. For example, if you will only ship to the contiguous US, you will want to remove Hawaii and Alaska from the list.

STEP BY STEP

1. In the Admin menu click the **States** link.

2. Make any modifications.

3. To add a new state, click the ⬛ button.

4. To edit a state, click the ⬛ button.

5. To remove a state, check the **Remove** box.

6. Click the **Update** button.

 The only time you would remove a state is if you will not accept orders or ship to that state. If you remove the Outside US option, only US customers will be able to checkout, and customers will be required to fill out both the Ship To and Bill To sections when they checkout even if they are the same.

Viewing, Modifying & Deleting Countries

Miva Merchant includes a list of nearly every country that can accept shipments. You may want to remove (or add) countries. For example, if there is a country you will not deliver to, or one you will not accept payment from, then you will want to remove that country from the list. You cannot add countries through the Miva Merchant Admin.

STEP BY STEP

1. In the Admin menu, click the **Countries** link.

2. Scroll through the list of countries, unchecking any country you do not want to use (this will only unassign them, so you can always reassign them later).

3. Click the **Update** button.

Remember: If you want to view more than 10 per page, enter a new number and then click the ⬛ button.

Order Minimums

You can require that customers order a minimum number of items or spend minimum dollar amount. If the minimum amount is not reached, the customer will be prompted with a message and will not be able to proceed to checkout.

Be careful when considering setting order minimums. If your reasoning for setting minimums is only because you want the customer to spend more money with you, consider instead giving the customer reasons to make additional purchases. Order minimums should only be used if you are unable to provide fulfillment unless a certain amount is reached. It's not for every online store.

If you require minimums, make sure you include information about this not only in a customer service section, but also on the home page of the site and store, and ideally as well somewhere in the store's template, so everyone is forewarned.

STEP BY STEP

---

1. In the Admin Menu, click your store name's link.

2. In the right-hand screen, click the **Order Minimums** link.

3. Enter your options: the **Minimum Quantity**, the **Minimum Price**, or enter amounts in both boxes.

4. If you entered an amount for both and want each order to meet both minimums, check off the **Must Meet Both Minimums** box. Otherwise, only one of the criteria will need to be met.

5. Enter content for the **Minimum Not Met Message**. This will appear to the customer when attempting to checkout if the minimum requirements are not met.

6. Click the **Update** button.

Setting Sales Tax or VAT

Miva Merchant includes a variety of tax and VAT modules. Only one option may be used for your Miva Merchant store.

If you reside in a state that uses different tax rates for each tax location or county, use the Shopper Selected Sales Tax option.

When you setup your Miva Merchant store, you set the method you will use. You'll find this selection by clicking your store name's link in the Admin Menu, then by clicking the Settings link on the right. If you need to change the method, do so here.

 If you setup tax options, then change the method under the Settings link, all configurations for the prior method will be lost.

After selecting your tax method, you'll need to configure the tax module.

STEP BY STEP   *W*

1. In the Admin Menu, click your store name's link.

2. Click the link on the right that pertains to the tax module you signified in the store's settings.

3. Configure the module according to your legal responsibilities.

   State Based Sales Tax
   For State Based Sales Tax, select whether the tax is applied to the state in the billing or shipping address.
   Click the ⬚ to add a state, then enter the tax rate for the state as a number (8.25 % would be entered as 8.25). Choose whether or not to tax the shipping (some states require this—check with tax offices first).

   Shopper Selected Sales Tax
   For Shopper Selected Sales Tax you will prompt the customer to choose their rate or location. For some states, this requires listing all tax locations or counties, which means you may have a lot of work ahead of you for this art. First, enter a label in the **Prompt** box, such as "Choose Your County."

   Click the ⬚ button to add each option. In the **Option** box, enter the label, such as the county or location name. In the **Rate** box enter the tax rate is a number (6.75% tax rate would be entered as simply 6.75). Choose whether or not to tax the shipping (some states require this—check with tax offices first).

4. Click the **Update** button.

PARENT CATEGORIES	CODE	NAME
BABY	BABY	Baby
	~~Baby~~ ᴮtops	Baby Tops
	~~BABY~~ᴮbritches (no space)	Baby Britches
	~~Baby~~ᴮouterwear	Baby Outwear
TODDLER	TODDLER	Toddler
	ᵀTtops	Toddler Tops
	ᵀTbritches	Toddler Britches
	ᵀouterwear	Toddler Outwear

Chapter Five

Categories & Products

Miva Merchant uses categories to organize products in the store. While you could just throw hundreds of products online without any categorization, it is ill advised. We've already discussed the importance of "ease of use" for your customers. Maintaining easy to navigate categories and subcategories is part of the process.

Before you start, you need to consider how many categories you will have. You can also use subcategories. It is suggested that you use no more than 12 main categories (five to seven top-level categories are ideal), as you don't want to confuse your customers with dozens of choices right off the bat. Use subcategories to break down the main categories.

Below is a sample hierarchical view of categories and subcategories.

The Music Store

Country
    Classic Country
    New Country

Rock
    Classic Rock
    Alternative Rock
    Hard Rock

Heavy Metal

Soundtracks

Clearance
    Music
      CDs
      Cassettes
    T-shirts

Pre-Order

BABY
TOPS
BRIT
OUTER

TODDLER
TOPS
BRIT
OUTER

By assigning products to categories, you make a shopper's browsing experience a more pleasant one. While shoppers can SEARCH for products, they can also BROWSE for a particular type of item they are looking for.

You can have many levels of categories and sub-categories. However, the more levels you have, the more space will be taken up by the category tree when shoppers reach that level, which means less space will be available for actual product viewing. This is because Miva Merchant's default category tree grows as each main category is clicked on.

Creating & Working With Categories

We'll start with adding a standard category. Later we'll talk about advanced options.

Creating Categories

STEP BY STEP   **W**

1. In the Admin Menu, click on the ▶ next to your store's named link.

2. Click on the ▶ next to **Categories**.

3. Click on **Add Category** and enter data for the main fields.

<table>
<tr>
<td>

Add Category

Category Pagination Headers & Footers Images

Category Code: COUNTRY
Category Name: Country Music
Parent Category: [   ] (H)
                          ☑ Active

</td>
<td>

Be Logical...
When creating category codes, try to use something logical, making it easier for you to reference if you later work with data files dealing with the codes rather than the category names.

Also, the code will appear in the browser's URL bar, which means it can be picked up by some search engines. To denote spaces in codes, use an underscore (_), as codes cannot contain actual spaces.

</td>
</tr>
</table>

Category Code – The unique code for the category. It can be an abbreviation (such as CY for Country), a word or even a group of words using underscores. You may only use letters, numbers, dashes and underscores. Do not use spaces or any special characters—Miva Merchant will reject them.

Category Name – The actual name of the category. The name can contain spaces, but be careful about using very long names.

Parent Category – If the category being created is a subcategory, you would enter the parent category code here. Leave this blank for now.

Active – If checked, the category will appear in the store, if not, then it will not be seen by potential customers (but will appear in the Admin area); you can temporarily turn categories off in your store.

4. Click on the **Pagination** link..

You can tell Miva Merchant how many products to display per page in each category. If you set this to 10 and there are 50 products in this category, visitors will get a Next button to move to the subsequent pages of products. The result will be five pages with 10 products on each page.

You may choose not to paginate. However, if there are many products in the category, the thumbnail images for those products will increase page load time. Our recommendation is that if you have more than 20 items in a category, you should paginate. Individual products will still load in their own pages.

5. Click on **Headers and Footers**.

> Headers and footers play a big role in an online store. For categories, they help you to provide overview information about a particular group of products.

Category	Pagination	**Headers & Footers**	Images

☑ Display Category Title

Header: `<p>From Johnny Cash to Garth Brooks, you'll find all of Country's greats right here.</p>`

`<b>Featured Items:</b>`

Footer:

> Here's where you can hype the product line, provide links to additional categories, or address frequently asked questions in description form.
>
> Category headers and footers can contain HTML, so you can format them as you wish.

Display Category Title – The category title is actually the category name, or a graphic you assign in place of the category name. It will be displayed *below* any category header, so if you are including a category header, you may want to put the category name within it, and uncheck the Display Category Title box.

6. Click on the **Add** button.

✔ Categories are the basis for product listings, so once you've added them, you can begin adding products to your store or make additional changes to any category itself. When creating a category, the only required information is the code, name and parent category (if applicable).

Using Images for Categories

You can opt to use an image rather than just text for the category listings in the category tree and in category titles (appearing on the actual category's page).

In order to use graphical navigation of categories, you first need to create the images. We recommend the following:

Category Tree:
A button (.gif) about 120-140 pixels wide by 20-25 pixels high. These buttons should all be the same width. They will appear in the left-frame of the category listings. Not all categories and sub-categories require images.

Category Title:
An image (.gif or .jpg) no larger than 300 pixels wide and 60 pixels high. These images will be displayed at the top of each category page which lists your products in that category. You don't want the image to take up too much of the screen; customers are there to shop.

 If you are not sure about specifications of images and graphics for the Web (size, file type, etc.), please review Appendix B before adding any images or custom graphics to your online store.

You can add the image as you add the category (by clicking the Images link at the top), or you can edit the category later.

Uploading Category Images

To upload a graphic for the category listing or category tree, click the ⬆ button next to the appropriate selection.

Click the **Browse...** button and navigate to the directory and file on your computer. When you find the file, double-click to return to this screen.

If the file already exists and you are uploading a new copy of it, check off **Overwrite** box. Otherwise, leave this unchecked.

Once the file name and path appears in the File box (it could take a few moments, depending on file size and your connection speed), click the **Upload** button.

Category	Pagination	Headers & Footers	**Images**

Tree Image: [   ] ⬆
Title Image: [   ] ⬆

Upload File - Microsoft Internet Explorer   _□×

Upload File

☐ **Overwrite**
File: [C:\Documents and Settings\Pamela\Deskto] Browse...

Upload   Cancel

Creating Sub-Categories

Sub-categories are great to further categorize your products. When a subcategory is created, the main category to which it assigned is called the **parent category**.

You can create a sub-category one of three ways:

◆ In the Category tree in the Admin Menu, click the ▶ next to the parent category, and then click on **Add Sub-Category**.

◆ In the Category tree in the Admin Menu, click on **Add Category**.

◆ In the Admin Menu, click on the **Categories** link and at the category sort list, click the button.

Category Code:	COUNTRY_NEW
Category Name:	New Country
Parent Category:	COUNTRY
	☑ Active

You enter information for sub-categories the same way you do for parent categories. The only difference is signifying the parent category (which will already be entered if you chose option 1 above).

✔ **The parent category is the category CODE, not the actual name of the category. The parent category must already exist in order for you to create a sub-category.**

If you need to look up the appropriate parent category, click the  button next to the parent category entry box. This will launch a pop-up window of all current categories. When you find the category you want, click the ⬆ button.

✔ *A category can be both a sub-category and a parent category, in this example, Women's is a subcategory Apparel (which is a parent category) and is also the parent category of Trousers. The Apparel category is only a parent category, and Trousers is only a subcategory.*

Apparel
   Women's
      Trousers
      Blouses

   Men's
      Slacks
      Shoes

Handbags

Editing Categories

Don't worry if you make a mistake on some of your category headers and footers, category names, parent category assignments, or other aspects. You can edit each and every one of your categories at any time by just clicking on the category name in the category list in the Admin Menu, making the changes, then clicking the **Update** button. The entry screens are identical to when you created the category.

Categories				
			Search: [ ]	
Sort:	Name Ascending Name Descending			
	Code Ascending Code Descending			
Remove	Code	Name	Active	
□	↓ COUNTRY	Country Music	✓	
□	↑↓ COUNTRY_CLASSIC	Classic Country	✓	
□	↑ COUNTRY_NEW	New Country	✓	
1-3			10	

From the category listing screen, you can edit the code, name or availability of a category by clicking the button (edit here). To edit other details of the category, click the button to launch the Edit Category screen.

To find a particular category, use the search box at the top of the screen.

You can also edit categories from the category tree in the Admin Menu. Just use the ▶ to navigate to the category you want to edit, then click the category name.

Deleting Categories

To delete a category, just go to the category in the Admin Menu, and click the **Delete** button.

Deleting a category will not delete the products within the category, but you will probably want to assign those products to other category. Otherwise shoppers won't see the products listed unless they navigate all the product listings, or perform a search with particular terms which will call that product to be listed. We'll learn how assign products to categories in a bit.

 After deleting items, the store's data files need to be packed. Refer to Chapter Eight: Store Maintenance.

Troubleshooting Category Codes

All Categories must have a unique Code. However, many categories can have the same Name. For example, if you sell apparel for both women and men and you want to use MEN and WOMEN as main categories and the types of apparel in subcategories, here's what you can do. In this example, we list the Name of the category, followed by the Code (unique identifier).

MEN (men)
    SHIRTS (m-shirt)
    PANTS (m-pants)
    TIES (m-ties)

WOMEN (women)
    SHIRTS (w-shirt)
    PANTS (w-pants)

By using a letter prefix in front of the base category code, it will be easier for you to distinguish which category you are working with in the Admin. This also helps when assigning category codes during the advanced feature of importing products via a flat file. This is just an example, as you could have also used wm- or women- as prefixes, so long as the category code is unique.

Sorting Categories

You can tell Miva Merchant how you want your categories to be ordered on the store pages. You can sort them alphabetically, by popularity or any other way you'd like, by Category Name or Category Code. You can also sort manually, even after sorting by name or code, so you can move specific categories to exact locations.

How you plan to sort may also play a role in how you code your categories. For example, if you prefix category codes with numbers, like 001-, 002-, etc, you can rely on the sort method in Miva Merchant to put them in the exact order you want.

To sort by Category Name or Code, simply click the appropriate links.

Manual sorting can be a tedious process if you have several categories.

STEP BY STEP

1. In the Admin Menu, click the **Categories** link.

2. Use the ⬆ and ⬇ buttons to reorder the categories.

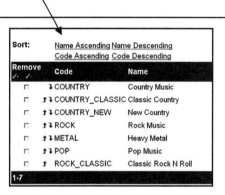

3. If necessary, click the yellow arrow at the bottom to move to the next page.

    If you want to view more than 10 items per page, enter a new number and a click the 🔄 button.

4. Click the **Update** button.

 If you want to sort by other methods, such as listing all newly added categories first, you will need to use a third-party module.

Creating & Working With Products

There's a long way, and a short way, to add products to your online store. We'll start with the long way, so you'll better understand just how products are assigned to the store.

It is wise to implement some sort of logical numbering or coding system for your products. This system should match any current inventory or invoicing program you may already have implemented, or you can create one as you build your store. Product codes can include numbers and letters dashes and underscores—you cannot use spaces or special characters.

Adding a Product

This first exercise explains how to create an uncategorized product. We can categorize it later.

STEP BY STEP   **W**
---

1. In the Admin Menu, click the ▶ next to **Products**.

2. Click the **Add Product** link.

3. Enter the **Product Code**. It must be unique.

```
┌─────────────────────────────────────────────────────────────┐
│ Add Product                                            [✏]   │
│                                                               │
│ Product  Images  Miva Marketplace  Headers & Footers          │
│ Product Code: [GB_DoubleLive]    ◄─────   The product code is a unique identifier. It can only
│ Product Name: [Garth Brooks: Double Live]    contain letters, numbers, dashes and underscores.
│ Category Code: [COUNTRY_NEW] (M)
│ Price:     [24.99]                         Some people simply number products (1001, 1002,
│ Cost:      [16.50]                         etc) while others use internal SKU numbers or create
│ Weight:    [.4]                            logical codes.
│ Description:  [eleased November 17, 1998, this double CD offers up a
│                reat selection of Garth's music. Featuring superior audio
│                uality.
│                ]
│                ☑ Taxable
│                ☑ Active
│                                                   [Add] [Reset]
└─────────────────────────────────────────────────────────────┘
```

4. Enter the **Product Name**. Be careful about making the product name too long. Simply state what the product is. You'll use a product description for details.

5. If you have already created the appropriate category, you may enter the **Category Code**, or click the (M) button and find the proper code. (If you haven't created the category yet, or if you'll list this in more than one category, you can always assign it later.)

6. Enter the retail price in the **Price** box. Do not include the $.

7. If desired, enter the **Cost** of the product.

The **Cost** box was designed to house your actual product cost, but it can be used for the wholesale price or a discount price you will offer to select customers. (If you'll only be offering a straight discount to select customers, and it will always be the same percentage, there's no need to enter the price here. If you have a **Cost** price, enter it here.)
Some third-party solutions also use this field to calculate savings or other pricing features. This will be discussed in more detail later.

8. If you will be figuring shipping charges based on **Weight**, enter the product's weight here. Be sure to use the same format as you did during Setup (pounds or ounces). You can enter fractional amounts—for ½ pound enter 0.5. If you will not be using the weight feature at all, leave this box at 0.00, as something must be entered.

 Versions 4.23 and higher will allow you suppress the weight from displaying. For prior versions, unless you have someone modify one of Miva Merchant's coded files, or install a module that removes it, the weight field will always be shown on your product pages.

9. Enter the **Description** for the product.

    Descriptions should include all information about the product. Since the SEARCH function does look in the description field, you should be sure to use any relative words you did not use in the title. (For example: from the movie Ghostbusters).

    Search engines also use the product description, so don't be afraid to go into great detail (your customers will thank you).

    The product description can include HTML, so feel free to use tags if you know them! Just be sure not to include the <HTML>, <HEAD> or <BODY> tags.

10. If the item is **Taxable**, leave this box checked. Otherwise, uncheck it.

11. By default this item will be **Active**, which means customers can view the product in the store. If you want to temporarily disable it, uncheck this box. You will still be able to see the product in the Admin area, but customers will not see it at all.

12. Click the **Images** link.

    Each product may or may not have an image. Any actual product (something that will be shipped to the customer) should have an image. An image will always help you sell the item.

    Thumbnail Image
    This is a small image which is displayed on the category pages, along with the product name, price and the "Add One" and "Buy Now" buttons. Visitors will click on this image or the product name to view a larger image and the product description.

     If you are using Miva Merchant Look and Feel in its standard format, then your thumbnails should all be the same width. If you are using KoolCat, or plan to use a third-party module to display the category pages horizontally, thumbnails should be the same height. Ultimately, creating each thumbnail with the same height and width will give you more display options. See Appendix B for more image information, including screenshots.

Full-Sized Image

This is the full image the customer sees on the product page, which also includes the product description and an option for a customer to enter how many they would like to buy.

 If you want to really keep track of things, name your full-sized images the product code (and file extension) and your thumbnail images the product code plus the letter "a" or "_small". Example: 1001.jpg, 1001a.jpg. Doing so can also help in the future with auto-calling images based on the product code—a feature utilized by some third-party modules.

To upload your product images, click the button next to the type of image you want to upload (thumbnail or full-sized).

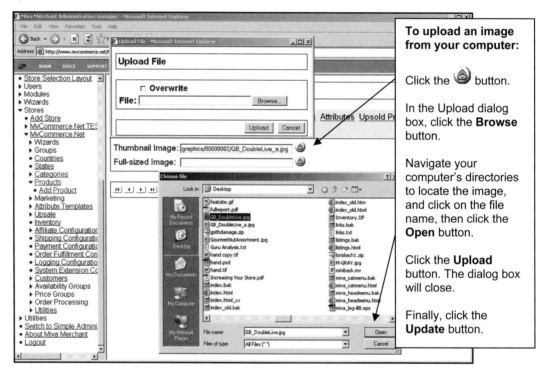

To upload an image from your computer:

Click the button.

In the Upload dialog box, click the **Browse** button.

Navigate your computer's directories to locate the image, and click on the file name, then click the **Open** button.

Click the **Upload** button. The dialog box will close.

Finally, click the **Update** button.

13. Click on the **Headers and Footers** link

> With a standard Miva Merchant store, all of your product information (description, image, price, weight, buy buttons, etc.) will appear in its own area on the page. Sometimes you may want additional text or images to appear above or below this area. This is where **product headers and footers** come into play.
>
> Product headers and footers work the same way as category headers and footers. You can use a product header to include special information (i.e. SALE! Buy One, Get One Free!!), or you may choose to use a footer to enter links or other information below the actual product area.

Example of product header.

Example of product footer.

> Headers and Footers are not required for individual products. Many stores don't use them. But if you want the customer to be hit with some big special or news on the product page (this will appear at the top, before the product), then this feature can come in handy.

14. Click on the **Add** button to save your product.

Custom Product Fields

> Miva Merchant version 4.23 boasted a new feature, allowing you to add Custom Fields to your products. These can be used to denote additional information, such as an ISBN number or publication year.
>
> To activate Custom Fields, in your Admin click the **Utilities** link, then check off the **Custom Fields** module, and click Update.
>
> To add fields (so you can later add information), click the **Custom Product Fields** link in the right-hand screen, and use the button to create fields.

Click the button to create new fields. Enter a Code and Name for each field.

Editing Products

Any of the fields you defined while adding a product can be edited. There are also additional product parameters that only become available after a product is added. These include attributes and related products.

STEP BY STEP

---

1. In the Admin Menu, click the **Products** link.

2. Enter the product code in the **Search Box** and click the 🔍 button.

> For quick edits, you can opt to display fields in the product listing. You can then use the 📄 button to edit individual fields right from this screen.

> **Products**
>
> [All] [Uncategorized]   Search: [   ] 🔍
>
> Display: ☑ Code   ☑ Name   ☑ Price
>   ☐ Cost   ☐ Weight   ☐ Description
>   ☐ Taxable ☐ Thumbnail Image ☐ Full-sized Image
>   ☐ Active
>
> Sort: Name Ascending Name Descending
>   Code Ascending Code Descending
>
> | Remove ✓ ✓ | Code | Name | Price 📄 |
> |---|---|---|---|
> | ☐ | GB_DoubleLive | Garth Brooks: Double Live | 24.99 📄 📄 |
> | 1-1 | | | 10 🔄 |

> To view more than 10 products at a time, change the number and click the refresh button.

 If you only need to change the name of the product, or any other item which is apparent in the product listing, then click the 📄 button (edit here).

You can choose what information is displayed in the product listings. By default this is the Name and Code of the product, but you can select from many other pieces of information.

3. Find the product you want to edit, then click the 📄 button to view a screen for product editing.

4. Make the changes to the product by clicking on each of the links at the top. Additional links will be displayed.

> | **Product** | Images | Related Products Attributes Upsold Products |
> |---|---|---|
> | Miva Marketplace | Headers & Footers | |

Related Products – products that are add-ons or related items to this product.

Attributes – lets you set different product attributes, such as size and color.

Upsold Products – additional products that will be offered as "upsell" items.

Inventory – the amount of this product you have on hand. This will only display if you've already activated the Inventory feature.

4x

Custom Fields – if you have already turned on this feature, you can add data for additional product fields.

5. We'll be discussing each of the features shortly. For now, if you made any changes, click the **Update** button to save them.

 If you ever make a mistake while editing a product, click the RESET button. This will revert the data back to its original form.

In Miva Merchant version 4.23 and higher you can tell Miva Merchant which elements of the product you would like displayed on the product screen. To set these options, in the Admin Menu, click your store name's link. In the right-hand screen, click the **Product Display Layout** link. Check or uncheck the various elements; use the pull-down menu to select options for the product image and inventory. When finished, click the **Update** button.

Assigning Related Products

Related Products allows you to display a list of "add-ons" to the potential customer directly on a product's page. This is useful for sites that sell accessories for items, or want to promote similar items on a specific product's page. By default, Related Products appear on the product page, below all of the product's information.

To assign a Related Product, both the original and related products must already be created.

STEP BY STEP

1. In the Admin menu, click on the **Products** link.

2. Find the main product which will house the related items, and click the button to launch the existing product's full edit window.

3. Click the **Related Products** link.

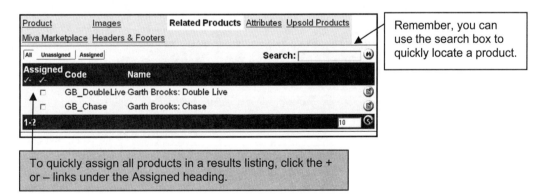

Remember, you can use the search box to quickly locate a product.

To quickly assign all products in a results listing, click the + or – links under the Assigned heading.

4. Find the product(s) you want to relate to this main product and **check the box** for each one.

5. Click the **Update** button.

If you view the product page on the front end, you'll now see additional items listed at the bottom of the screen.

Remember, you will need to refresh the browser's window to view the changes.

You can later unassign any related products by simply unchecking the assigned box.

Related Products Layout

You can tell Miva Merchant how to layout related products and which fields to display. In the Admin Menu, click your store's link. On the right, click **Related Products Layout**. Set your options then click the **Update** button.

Assigning Products to Categories

Unless you assign the Category Code while adding products, your store's products will only be available via searching or by viewing the complete product list. Products will never be listed within categories until they are assigned.

STEP BY STEP

---

1. In the Admin Menu, click the ▶ next to **Categories**.

2. Click on the name of the category to which you want to assign products.

3. Click the **Products** link at the top of this category's Admin screen.

4. Using the product list, or by searching, put a **check** next to each product that should be assigned to the category.

5. Click the **Update** button.

Filtering Products Before Assigning

When you click on the Assigned button, only products already assigned to the category will be listed (they will have a check mark). Hence, when you click the Unassigned button, only products that are not assigned to the category will be listed. You can also use the search field on this screen to search for specific products that have or have not been assigned to a particular category.

> In our country store, if we want to find any Garth Brooks products that are not yet assigned, we first click the __Unassigned__ button, then perform a search for Garth. The only results will be those matching the term "Garth" that have not yet be assigned to the category.

Locating Unassigned Products

You can easily locate any products that are not assigned to a category. This is useful since you want to make sure that nearly all products in your store are assigned to at least one category. We recommend performing this task on a regular basis to make sure you don't have any hanging products.

STEP BY STEP

1. In the Admin Menu, click the **Products** link.

2. At the top of the product listing, click the __Uncategorized__ button.

Assigning Products to Several Categories

You can tell Miva Merchant to display a product in a realm of categories. Cross-referencing is a great feature, because products only have to be entered once, and customers will be able to find it in various locations.

When cross-referencing, keep in mind that products should only be assigned to categories to which they belong.

To assign products to more than one category, simply follow the same instructions as assigning a product to any one category. There is no need to create the same product with different codes.

 There is a much quicker way to assign products to categories; it is done by importing a file. Once you become more familiar with the products pages and how products are handled by Miva Merchant, you can consider using the import feature, discussed later.

Deleting Products

You can delete a product at its edit screen. It doesn't matter how you reach this screen (through the products list, categories list, search, etc.). Just click the **Delete** button.

 There is no immediate un-do feature. The only way to get a product back is to have someone edit your store's product's database before you do anything else.

You can also delete products from the product listing screen. In the Admin Menu, click the **Products** link. In the **Remove** column, check off any products you want to delete, then click the **Update** button.

Remove ✓- ✓-		Code	Name
□	↓	GB_DoubleLive	Garth Brooks: Double Live
□	↑	GB_Chase	Garth Brooks: Chase
1-2			

 After deleting items, the store's data files need to be packed. Refer to Chapter Eight: Store Maintenance.

Sorting Products

By default, products are sorted in the order in which they are entered into the store. You can manipulate the order in which products are displayed on the category, search and product list screens. You can sort them alphabetically, by popularity or any other way you'd like, by Product Name or Product Code. You can also sort manually, even after sorting by name or code, so you can move specific products to exact locations.

Manual sorting can be a tedious process if you have several products.

STEP BY STEP
---

1. In the Admin Menu, click the **Products** link.

2. Use the ↑ and ↓ buttons to move the products to the proper order.

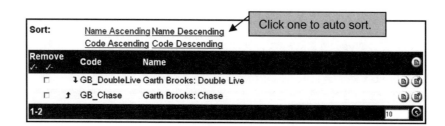

You can also use the **Ascending** and **Descending** links to sort by product name or code.

3. If necessary, click the yellow arrow at the bottom of the screen to move to the next page of product listings. Or, enter a larger number of listings to display on this screen and click the ⟳ button.

4. Click the **Update** button.

For more robust sorting options, consider using a third-party module.

Product Attributes & Options

You might have products that vary in size, color or weight. For example, if you sell T-shirts, you might have ones that come in Small, Medium and Large, as well as different colors.

It is counterproductive to produce a single product page for each of these shirts. It may also confuse potential customers.

> **Attributes allow you to offer various sizes, colors or styles of a product without forcing the customer to search for his or her size or other variations of the product.**

By using Attributes, you can create one product (the shirt) and prompt the user to select the size they would like to order. Attributes and options can also call for an increase in price.

Types of Attributes

Miva Merchant offers five different types of attribute listings. They are:

Radio Buttons
The customer is presented with a list of options on the screen, and they click a circle for the option he/she wants. With this type of attribute, the customer may only select one of the options.

Drop-down List
The customer is presented with a pull-down menu that lists all the options. The customer clicks the option he/she wants. With this type of attribute, the customer may only select one of the options.

Checkbox
An option is presented, preceded by a checkbox. The customer checks the box if he/she wants the option. This type of attribute can also be used to require an add-on or an agreement.

Text Field
The customer enters text in a one-line text box. This attribute type is useful for collecting brief information, such as the slogan a customer wants printed on a shirt.

Text Area
The customer enters text in a several-line text box. This attribute type is useful for collecting messages or comments from the customer.

Spec Out the Attributes and Options

Before creating attributes for your products, you should sit down and figure out how you will offer the products. If you're just selling shirts in different sizes, this is quite simple, as is selling shirts in different colors. However, if the shirts have different sizes and different colors, how will you offer them?

Our example is of a T-shirt, which is available in different sizes and colors. Without any attributes, we are offering a plain white Tee to the customer. Our base price here is $8.00.

Our first step is to determine how we are going to present the options. For our sizes and colors, we can use a **List Select** option, which presents a pull-down menu to the potential customer, or **Radio Buttons**, which show all options on the screen immediately and one is selected by clicking a button.

When creating attributes in Miva Merchant, the attributes may or may not be supported by additional options. In our example later in this section, the size of a T-shirt is an attribute, and the various sizes (L, XL, etc.) are the options we created.

Standard Crew Neck Tee
Quantity in Basket: *none*
Code: **TEE_Standard**
Price: **$8.00**
Shipping Weight: **0.10** pounds
Quantity: [1]   [Add To Basket]
Our standard T-shirt is made of 100% pre-shrunk cotton. Available in various sizes and colors.

Attributes will help sell like products in several sizes or colors. The customer won't have to weed through a long list to find the one to buy.

Which list-select format do I use?

Radio buttons work well if you have only three to four options. For many options, consider using the Drop-down List format.

Don't worry if you created one method and want to switch later. You can switch from List Select to Radio Buttons, and vice versa, in the click of a button.

Negative Amounts

You can enter negative amounts for attributes and options. For example, if you sell computers and want to subtract a dollar amount if the customer opts to not accept a certain option (such as a monitor), you can do so. Simply include the minus sign (-) before the amount.

Creating List-Select Attributes

Our example here offers this Tee in L, XL and XXL, and in the colors white, navy, red, green and orange. Obviously, we don't want to create 15 different products (3 sizes x 5 colors). So we use attributes. We can provide a pull-down menu or for shoppers to tell us which color and size they would like to purchase.

STEP BY STEP

1. Open the product for editing.

2. Click on the **Attributes** link.

3. Click on the ⓓ button to create a new attribute for this product.

> **Edit Product: Standard Crew Neck Tee**
>
> Product   Images   Related Products **Attributes** Upsold Products
> Miva Marketplace Headers & Footers
>
> | Code | Prompt | Image | Type | Copy? | Price | Cost | D | R | ⓓ |
> |------|--------|-------|------|-------|-------|------|---|---|---|
> | | | ⓐ | Radio Buttons ▾ | ☐ | 0.00 | 0.00 | ☐ | | |
>
> ⮜⮜ ⮜ ⮞ ⮞⮞   Update Delete Reset

4. Enter a **Code** for the attribute. Customers will see this code on the basket and order screens, as well as in their confirmation e-mail. You should make it something they will understand, such as SIZE or COLOR. Remember, no spaces or special characters in codes.

> ✔ *Unlike product and category codes, attribute codes are assigned per product and must only be unique for the individual product. You can use the same attribute code for one product as you do another. You cannot, however, use a duplicate attribute code within the same product.*

5. In the **Prompt** box, type the label you want the customer to see on the product page, such as "Choose Color." If this option will carry an additional cost, include that information, as Miva Merchant does not automatically display it on the screen.

6. If desired, upload an image that will appear in place of the Prompt text.

7. In the **Type** list, use the pull-down menu to select the type of attribute you want to use. For a listing of options, choose either **Radio Buttons** or **Drop-down List**.

8. Check off whether or not the attribute is **Required** (noted as "R"). In our example it is required, because we have to know what size shirt the customer wants. If your list or other type of attribute is solely for add-on purposes, then you would not check this option.

9. Click the **Update** button.

> Your initial information will be saved, and a new row of input boxes will appear, these are for the available options of this attribute.

10. Enter the **Code** for the first attribute option (in our case, the size of the shirt). The customer will see this on their order, so make it simple, such as "Large."

11. Enter the **Prompt** for the attribute option – this is what will appear in the actual drop-down list or next to the radio buttons. Include the additional price if there is one. For example "XX-Large – add $2."

12. If you are using Radio Buttons, you can upload an image that will appear for each selection. The image feature will not work for the Drop-down List options.

Code	Prompt	Image	Type	Copy?	Price	Cost	D R	
SIZE	Choose Size		Radio Buttons	N/A	N/A		✓	
↧ L	Large				0.00	0.00		
↥↧ XL	X-Large				0.00	0.00		
↥ XXL	XX-Large - add $2				2.00	1.00		
					0.00	0.00		

13. Enter the **Price** which will be added to the product because this option was selected. (in our case, 1.00).

14. If you want this to be the default option, check the **Default** checkbox (noted in column heading "D."

   Default options are options automatically selected by default. For Radio Buttons listings, the default item will automatically be selected. For Drop-down Lists, it will also be selected, and will be the only option the customer sees unless he/she pulls down the menu.

15. Click the **Update** button.

16. Repeat steps 10-15 for each related attribute (appearing on the pull-down or radio menu) for this particular list.

When you've completed adding your first attribute, reload the product page on the front end to view the changes.

Since, in our example, we'll also be prompting for the color of the shirt, we'll create a totally new attribute list by clicking the 🔳 button at the very top of the attribute screen. Then we'll create our new list just as we did for the T-shirt size.

Standard Crew Neck Tee

Quantity in Basket: *none*
Code: **TEE_Standard**
Price: **$8.00**
Shipping Weight: **0.10** pounds

Choose Size: ○ Large
                  ○ X-Large
                  ○ XX-Large - add $2
Choose Color: Red ▾
Enter Slogan: [   ]
                  □ Include a sample cap with my slogan - add $9

Quantity: [1]   Add To Basket

Our standard T-shirt is made of 100% pre-shrunk cotton. Available in various sizes and colors.

Creating Text Field Attributes

Text fields are one-line fields. Use them to obtain brief information, such as names or four-eight word instructions.

STEP BY STEP *W*

1. Open the product for editing.

2. Click on the **Attributes** link.

3. Click the button to create a new attribute.

4. Enter the **Code** and **Prompt** for the Attribute, and select **Text-Entry Field** from the pull-down menu. If this option will carry an additional cost, include that information, as Miva Merchant does not automatically display it on the screen.

   ✔ *Unlike product and category codes, attribute codes are assigned per product and must only be unique for the individual product. You can use the same attribute code for one product as you do another. You cannot, however, use a duplicate attribute code within the same product.*

5. Enter the additional **Price** (if applicable).

6. If you want to include an Image (to replace the prompt text), then click the 🖻 button.

7. Choose whether the information needs to be **Required** or not by using the checkbox under the column heading "R."

8. Click on the **Update** button.

Creating Text Area Attributes

If you want to collect more detailed information, such as complete sentences or lengthy instructions, choose this option.

STEP BY STEP *W*

1. Open the product for editing.

2. Click on the **Attributes** link.

3. Click the button to create a new attribute.

4. Enter the **Code** and **Prompt** for the Attribute, and select **Text Area** from the pull-down menu. If this option will carry an additional cost, include that information, as Miva Merchant does not automatically display it on the screen.

   ✔ *Unlike product and category codes, attribute codes are assigned per product and must only be unique for the individual product. You can use the same attribute code for one product as you do another. You cannot, however, use a duplicate attribute code within the same product.*

5. Enter the additional **Price** (for this item above, there is no additional price).

6. If you want to include an **Image** (to replace the prompt text), then click the button.

MESSAGE	Enter Gift Message		graphics/0000000	Text Area

7. Choose whether the information needs to be **Required** or not by using the checkbox under column heading "R."

8. Click on the **Update** button.

Creating "Check-off" Attributes

You can also ask customers to check or uncheck certain product options. This can be used as a "do you want this?" option, or as a required acknowledgement (such as a license agreement).

STEP BY STEP ⅥⅣ

1. Open the product for editing.

2. Click on the **Attributes** link.

3. Click the 🅳 button to create a new attribute.

4. Enter the **Code** and **Prompt,** and choose the **Checkbox** option from the pull-down menu. If this option will carry an additional cost, include that information, as Miva Merchant does not automatically display it on the screen.

> ✔ *Unlike product and category codes, attribute codes are assigned per product and must only be unique for the individual product. You can use the same attribute code for one product as you do another. You cannot, however, use a duplicate attribute code within the same product.*

5. If you want to use an **Image** in place of the prompt, click the button.

6. Enter the additional cost to the customer in the **Price** field (if applicable).

7. If the attribute is required check the **Required** box under column heading "R."

8. Click the **Update** button.

Attribute Example

In our example product's attributes, we prompt the customer for the size and color, ask them to enter their slogan, and offer a sample cap with their slogan on it for $9 additional. We also charge an additional $2 for all XX-Large shirts, because they are more expensive.

Remove	Code	Prompt	Image	Type	Copy?	Price	Cost	D	R
□	SIZE	Choose Size		Radio Buttons	N/A	N/A		✓	
□	L	Large				0.00	0.00		
□	XL	X-Large				0.00	0.00		
□	XXL	XX-Large - add $2				2.00	1.00		
□	COLOR	Choose Color		Drop-down List	N/A	N/A		✓	
□	RED	Red				0.00	0.00		
□	GRAY	Gray				0.00	0.00		
□	BLACK	Black				0.00	0.00		
□	WHITE	White				0.00	0.00		
□	GREEN	Green				0.00	0.00		
□	BLUE	Blue				0.00	0.00		
□	YELLOW	Yellow				0.00	0.00		
□	SLOGAN	Enter Slogan		Text Field		0.00	0.00	✓	
□	CAP	Include a sample cap with my slogan - add $9		Checkbox		9.00	4.28		

Notice that on the XXL option and the Cap checkbox attribute, we included the words "add $X." This is because Miva Merchant, by default, will not automatically display this information.

Next, we go to the product page on our front end and refresh the screen to see the changes.

Standard Crew Neck Tee

Quantity in Basket: *none*
Code: **TEE_Standard**
Price: **$8.00**
Shipping Weight: **0.10** pounds

Choose Size: ○ Large
○ X-Large
○ XX-Large - add $2
Choose Color: [Red ▾]
Enter Slogan: [   ]
□ Include a sample cap with my slogan - add $9

Quantity: [1] [Add To Basket]

Our standard T-shirt is made of 100% pre-shrunk cotton. Available in various sizes and colors.

Editing Attributes and Options

Just as we created attributes, we can edit them. We can also add new selections to our attribute lists. To edit any attribute, just open the product for editing, click on the **Attributes** link, and then click the edit button. Make any changes, and click the **Update** button.

You can also sort your attributes and the options. Just use the ⬆ and ⬇ buttons as you do when sorting products.

Deleting Attributes and Options

To delete an attribute, open the product for editing, and click on the **Attributes** link.

In the list of attributes, check off any boxes under the Remove column, then click the **Update** button.

The attribute will be removed. The product, and any other attributes for that product, will remain intact.

Optionally, you can also use the check box field to remove an attribute and/or its options.

 Clicking the delete button at the bottom of the screen will delete the entire product.

After deleting items, the store's data files need to be backed. Refer to Chapter Eight: Store Maintenance.

Creating Attribute Templates 4x

Sometimes you might want to assign the same attribute (and options) to several products. Miva Merchant's Attribute Templates allows you to create a template attribute and assign that template to various products.

For example, if all T-shirts come in the same sizes, Attribute Templates will save a tremendous amount of time. We can create the template once, then apply it to all the products.

STEP BY STEP

1. In the Admin menu, click the **Attributes Template** link.

2. Click the button to create a new template.

3. Enter a **CODE** for the template. Remember, no spaces or special characters can be used.

4. Enter a template **PROMPT** - make it one that you will remember so you can quickly make assignments to products later.

5. Click the **Add** button.

   You will automatically be taken you to the Edit Attribute Templates screen.

6. Click the **Attribute and Options** link.

7. Click the button to create the options. This will be done the same way as for individual products.

8. Click the **Update** button when complete.

Assigning Attribute Templates **4X**

1. In the Admin Menu, find the product you want to assign the Attribute Template to. You will need to open the product for editing.

2. At the top of the product's edit screen, click the **Attributes** link.

3. Click the ⓓ button to create an attribute.

4. In the **Type** field, use the pull-down menu and select the template you want to use. It will be listed at the bottom of the list.

5. If you want to merely copy the Attribute Template to this product, check off the **Copy** box.

    By default, when an Attribute Template is modified, the change will be reflected on all the products to which it is assigned. Checking off the Copy box allows you to apply the template without it being bound to the template. If the template is later modified, the changes will not be reflected on any products where the Copy box was checked.

6. Click the **Update** button.

Editing Attribute Templates

To edit an attribute template, click the Attribute Templates link in the Admin Menu. After locating the template you want to edit, click the ⓔ button. To modify the attributes and options, click the **Attributes and Options** link.

Any products using the template will automatically be updated unless you opted to only copy the attribute template to the product.

Inventory Management

Miva Merchant's Inventory feature allows you to set and track inventory levels on your products. Inventory specifications can be set store-wide or individually for each product.

 The built-in inventory feature in version 4.x does not track inventory on product attributes.

Configuring the Store's Inventory Feature

The following will allow you to set a default inventory control for all products in the store.

STEP BY STEP

---

1. In the Admin Menu, click the **Inventory** link.

2. Check the **Track Inventory** box. Inventory will not be tracked unless the box is checked.

3. Set the parameters to signify how you want Inventory to be handled. You can use **tokens** to call in the product name, product code and stock level information (see next page).

Inventory Settings Email Notification

☐ Track Inventory
In Stock Message (Short): In Stock
In Stock Message (Long): %inv_instock% available for immediate delivery

Tokens are shorthand representatives of specific information. They are used within template messages.

☐ Track Low Stock Level
Low Stock Level: 0
Low Stock Message (Short): Backordered
Low Stock Message (Long): Please Note: '%product_name%' is currently backordered. Pl

For example, the token %product_name% will automatically display the name of the product.

☐ Track Out of Stock Level
☐ Hide Out of Stock Products
Out of Stock Level: 0
Out of Stock Message (Short): Sold Out
Out of Stock Message (Long): Sorry, we are currently sold out of '%product_name%'. Plea

Miva Merchant displays the available tokens at the bottom of the screen.

Limited Stock Message: Sorry, we do not have enough '%product_name%' to fill your

Some third-party modules, as well as the OpenUI, allow you to utilize tokens extensively.

Available Tokens: %product_name% The product's name
%product_code% The product's code
%inv_instock% The quantity in stock (current stock - low stock level)
%inv_available% The quantity available to buy (current stock - out of stock level)
%inv_level% The current stock level code: in, low, or out

In Stock Message (Short) – the short message displayed for inventory levels.

In Stock Message (Long) – the long message displayed for inventory levels.

Track Low Stock Level – to track the level of inventory when it is getting low, check this box.

Low Stock Level – enter the level (quantity) for which inventory is considered to be low.

Low Stock Message (Short) – the short message displayed for low inventory levels.

Low Stock Message (Long) – the long message displayed for low inventory levels.

Track Out of Stock Level – to track when an item is out of stock, check this box.

Hide Out of Stock Products – checking this will hide products from the customer if they are out of stock.

Out of Stock Level – usually zero, this is the quantity which the store considers means "out of stock."

Out of Stock Message (Short) – the short message displayed when an item is out of stock.

Out of Stock Message (Long) – the long message displayed when an item is out of stock.

Limited Stock Message – the message displayed when a customer orders more of one item than you have set in the inventory count.

Using Tokens for Messages

Tokens are "key codes" that can be used to automatically insert information, such as the product's name, code, quantity in stock, out of stock level and current stock level codes. They work similar to how data fields in a mail merge file function. These codes are useful in customizing the messages displayed.

Miva Merchant includes the following tokens for the Inventory feature:

> **%product_name%** - inserts the name of the product
> **%product_code%** - inserts the product code
> **%inv_instock%** - displays in stock quantity of the product as a number only
> **%inv_available%** - displays the available quantity of the product as a number only
> **%inv_level%** - displays the current stock level code (in, low, or out)

You can choose whether to display the long or short messages on product pages and other screens.

If you want the short message displayed on the product list screen in the format of "X Available Now," you would put:

%inv_instock% Available Now

If you wanted a longer message on the product screen, you could format it like this:

4. Click the **Email Notification** link.

5. If you want to be notified by email when inventory counts are low, or items are out of stock, enter the parameters.

> **Send Email When Stock is Low** – sends an email when the stock level reaches the Low quantity you previously specified.
>
> **Send Email When Stock is Out** - sends an email when an item is considered to be Out of Stock.
>
> **From** – enter the email address you want the message sent from (this will usually be your own address).
>
> **To** – enter the email address you want the message sent to (usually you or your purchasing department.
>
> **CC** – enter an alternative carbon copy email, such as purchasing or a drop ship house.
>
> **Subject** – enter the subject of the email message. You can use the codes (tokens) at the bottom of the screen to customize it per product and levels.
>
> **Email Message** – edit and tailor the email message as needed, using codes at the bottom.

6. When finished making all changes, click the **Update** button.

Assigning Inventory Counts to Products

Once you have set the default configuration for your store's inventory management, you may want to make some changes to specific products. In fact, you'll need to tell Miva Merchant which products should have their inventory tracked.

STEP BY STEP

---

1. In the Admin Menu, click on the **Products** link.

2. Find the product you want to set the inventory level on, and click the 🖱️ button to edit the product.

3. Click the **Inventory** link. If this link does not appear in your product's edit screen, then you failed to turn on the Inventory feature properly.

Just turning on the Inventory feature in Miva Merchant does not automatically set all products to have inventory tracked. You have to assign each product. There are quicker ways we discuss in the advanced section of this book.

You can increase and decrease stock levels here, and set a message to be displayed when an item is in stock and is not low in quantity. You may wish to leave this blank.

You can set low- and out-of-stock level options for individual products, or choose to use the default options you set.

4. Set the parameters according to how you want to handle the inventory on this particular product.

   Just as with the store's default settings, you can use Tokens to customize the messages.

5. When finished, click the **Update** button.

Allowing Backorders

You can allow customers to backorder items in the store. To do this, you must set the Out of Stock level for the product(s) as a negative number, such as -100. This will produce a message similar to this:

Please Note: 'PRODUCT NAME' is currently backordered.
Please be aware that there may be a delay in shipping.

Customers will still be able to add this item to their basket, so its recommended that you use this option wisely, and set it per product as needed. This will avoid taking backorders on items you may never receive again.

Troubleshooting the Inventory Feature

Miva Merchant's Inventory feature is not foolproof. When customers add items to their basket, the quantity of the product in the basket is held for the customer, and the actual inventory will decrement. If the customer removes the item from the basket, the inventory will be restocked. However, if the customer leaves the store, the inventory will continue to be "held" until one of three things happens:

♦ Expired Baskets are Deleted (and the store packed)

♦ You manually change the inventory

♦ You import new inventory

Even with a third-party module, it is virtually impossible to have a 100% inventory count 100% of the time. Just like in a grocery store, if you put an item in your basket, no one else can buy it until you let it go. And if you leave it at the front checkout counter, it must be placed back on the shelf before someone can see that it is again available.

Chapter Six

Customer Management and Salability

Now that you've created the shell of your online store, how will you manage customers? Do you want to be able to obtain and maintain contact information? What about making it easier for customers to checkout in the future?

Have you thought about targeting specific products or special prices to any existing customers? What if you want to have a "customer appreciation week," where all or some of your existing customers can take advantage of special discounts?

> **THIS WEEK ONLY!!**
>
> **20% off to all registered customers**

Maybe you also sell wholesale, and need to be able to offer special prices or discounts to storefront retailers.

You can assign customers to specific groups in order to do just these things.

Customer Accounts

Miva Merchant includes a **Customer Account** feature that allows customers to create a login to your store. Customers can then later take advantage of special offers, select items, and have their billing and shipping contact information automatically entered for them.

When we initially setup the store, we told Miva Merchant how to handle customer accounts in respect to providing login links and account creation pages. With this feature already implemented, we can begin managing our customers and offer various prices and products to those who register. If you opted to not utilize customer accounts, you can either skip this section, or re-enact this feature (see Chapter Four: Creating the Store).

Viewing Customer Accounts

When you click the **Customers** link in the Admin Menu, the following screen will appear. Any customer who created an account with your store will be listed here.

The customers screen displays information about all customers who have created an account. Without customization, you can't force customers to create an account, so obviously not all of those who have shopped your store will be listed.

To view all the details of the customer, locate the customer then click the ▣. You will be able to review everything except for the customer's password.

> *To view additional information in the standard customer list, you can check the boxes in the Display area. Usually you'll want to view the Login, E-mail, First Name and Last Name. After checking the options you want, click the Update button at the bottom of the screen.*

Creating Customer Accounts

While Miva Merchant gives the customer or potential customer the opportunity to create his or her own account, you may have some existing customers for whom you want to create the accounts for now.

If you're just starting to build your store, your customer list will be empty. We suggest you create a test account with your own information. You can use this to place test orders in your store later.

STEP BY STEP

1. In the Admin Menu, click the **Customers** link.

```
Add Customer                                    [ ]

Identification  Shipping/Billing Information
Login:                   testaccount
Email Lost Passwords To: test@test.com
Password:                ••••••
Confirm Password:        ••••••

                                        Add    Reset
```

2. Click the ⬛ button to create a new customer account.

3. Enter the **Login** name, **e-mail address** and create a **password** for the customer. The login name can be letters, numbers, underscores and dashes. It cannot contain spaces or special characters. You will need to retype the password to confirm accuracy.

4. If want to have the customer enter his or her own shipping and billing contact information when they login the first time, then just click the **Add** button. Otherwise, go to the next step.

5. Click the **Shipping/Billing Information** link.

6. Enter the customer's information.

7. Click the **Add** button.

✔ *Don't worry if you forgot to write down the password in a safe place. Your customer need only request an e-mailed password from your store's login page. Provided your mail server is configured properly, and the speed of connection and internet activity at the time, the customer should receive the e-mail from the store in a matter of seconds.*

Editing Customer Information

When viewing the customers list, next to each customer's information are two buttons.

The ⊟ button allows you to edit only the information shown in the listing (in our example, just the Login, E-mail, and First and Last Names). Clicking this button will make the fields for the particular customer editable.

The ⊟ button will launch a new window containing access to all of the customer's information.

STEP BY STEP

1. In the Admin Menu, click the **Customers** link.

2. Find the customer's listing you want to edit. You may have to navigate through the listings or use the search box.

3. Click the ⊟ button to launch a new window with the customer's information.

4. The only information you should usually consider changing on the **Identification** screen is the e-mail address. Since most customers create their own login and password (and can have any lost passwords e-mailed to them via the store), you should not change this information unless a customer requests you do so.

5. Click the **Shipping/Billing Information** link.

6. Here you can edit the customer's phone/fax numbers, company name, and shipping or billing addresses.

7. Since no payment information is stored in this area, you won't have access to view or change this type of information.

8. Once all changes have been made, click the **Update** button. If you have made no changes, or do not want to save your changes, click the **Reset** button.

Deleting Customers

You may decide you want to delete certain customers. The reasons for this will vary, but common ones are inactivity, falsely providing payment information and customers who attempt to "take you for a ride."

Deleting customers, of course, is not foolproof. Unless you install a customization that blocks specific IP addresses or cookies, visitors can simply create another account.

STEP BY STEP

1. In the Admin Menu, click the **Customers** link.

2. Find the customer you want to remove from the account list and check the **Remove** box.

3. Click the **Update** button.

You can also click the button to pull up the customer and click the **Delete** button.

✔ *After deleting a customer, you will be taken to an Add Customer screen, which will allow you to re-add the customer. However, you will need to enter a new password. If you do not want to re-add the customer, or add another customer simply move on to another task.*

Assigning Customer Fields

When customers create an account or checkout through the store, they are prompted to enter specific ship-to and bill-to information. By default, they are required to enter their first and last names, email address, phone number and shipping address. If the item is being shipped to a different person, they are also prompted to enter all the same fields for the billing address. The shipping information is required, but the billing information can be hidden if you desire.

Why would I hide the billing information? If you will only ship to the person placing the order, you might want to turn off the separate bill-to section.

You can make individual customer fields required, hidden or optional.

STEP BY STEP
---

1. In the Admin Menu, click on your store name's **link**.

2. Click the **Customer Fields** link.

Billing Information: Optional ▼

Field	Hidden	Required	Optional
First Name	○	●	○
Last Name	○	●	○
Email Address	○	●	○
Phone Number	○	●	○
Fax Number	○	○	●
Company	○	○	●
Address	○	●	○
City	○	●	○
State/Province	○	●	○
Zip/Postal Code	○	●	○
Country	○	●	○

3. Using the **radio buttons**, assign the proper requirement method to each field.

4. Choose for the **Billing Information** to be optional or hidden. If optional, the customer will only need to fill it out if the shipping and billing addresses are different. If hidden, the customer will only complete the Ship-To section, which requires all items to be shipped and billed to the same address.

 You cannot make fields optional in the Ship-To and required in the Bill-To, nor vice versa. Fields are either hidden, required or optional for both sections.

5. Click the **Update** button.

Availability Groups

Sometimes you may want to offer select items as an exclusive to particular customers. There are several reasons a store might offer such exclusives, including:

♦ You want your existing customers to get "first dibs" on new or rare product.

♦ The items might be "wholesale only," so you want to offer them just to retailers at a wholesale cost.

♦ You want to offer your best customers an item that is scarce, or hard to find.

♦ You run a membership club, whereas only club members can purchase certain items.

♦ You also want to run an employee store, making certain products available only to employees. Many corporations use availability groups for this purpose.

♦ You want someone else, such as a vendor or co-worker, to review the product listing in the store before making it available to the public.

With **Availability Groups**, you can make these selected items invisible to any customer who is not included in the group.

Customers assigned to an availability group must first log in. Otherwise, they will not see the additional options.

There's a specific process in creating and utilizing Availability Groups:

1. Create the group.

2. Assign the product(s) and/or categories.

3. Assign the customer(s) who you want to be able to view the products and/or categories that are part of the group.

Creating the Availability Group

1. In the Admin Menu, click the ▶ next to **Availability Groups**.

2. Click on the **Add Availability Group** link.

3. Enter the name of the **Availability Group**.

4. You can name the group whatever you'd like. Your customers will not see this name – it is for administrative purposes only.

5. Click the **Add** button.

Add Availability Group

Availability Group

Availability Group Name: Members Only

Add   Reset

Editing Availability Groups

After creating an Availability Group, you will automatically be taken to the Edit Availability Group area. This is where you will assign customers and products, as well as any special categories.

You can also reach this area any time by navigating to this group's name in the Admin Menu. Just click the ▶ next to **Availability Groups**, then the link of the group you want to edit.

STEP BY STEP

1. In the **Edit Availability Group** screen, click the **Customers** link.

2. Check off all the customers you want to assign to this group.

    When editing an existing group, you can click the Assigned *button to remove any customers, or the* Unassigned *button to add customers who are not yet assigned to the group.*

3. Click the **Update** button.

4. Click the **Categories** link.

You can choose (check off) to assign an entire category to the Availability Group. This means that only when customers assigned to the group are logged in they will see the category link. Any customer who is not logged in, or any customer who is not assigned to the Availability Group will not see the category link.

To further navigate this list, use the yellow arrow at the bottom of the screen, or use the **Search** feature.

Even if the products you want to assign are in this category you must assign products to the group as well. Otherwise, any shopper could find (and buy) the product during an item search.

5. Select any Categories to assign to this Availability Group then click the **Update** button.

6. Click the **Products** link.

    You can select specific products for this Availability Group the same way you selected categories. If you decide to select just products and no specific categories, assigned customers will only see these products **within the categories** they are assigned to (or in the product listing or search results) through the actual store.

    To add all products at once, choose to view more than 10 per page, then use the + button in the Assigned column to select them all at once.

    As with the customers area, if you ever want to add or remove categories in this Availability Group, you can navigate quickly using the **Assigned** or **Unassigned** buttons.

> *If you assign a category to a group of customers, and do not assign the products within that category, other shoppers will still be able to find those products in a Search on your store. Therefore, if you only want the assigned customers to see specific products within an assigned category, you must assign both the category and the products.*

7. Once you've made all your changes/additions, click the **Update** button.

Deleting Availability Groups

Once you are finished offering specific groups of items to select customers, or if you've made a mistake, you can delete the **Availability Group**.

STEP BY STEP
---

1. In the Admin Menu, click the ▶ next to **Availability Groups**.

2. Click on the link to the group you want to delete.

3. Click the Delete button.

[handwritten notes:]

ties into pending App'l module

FOR TB // AVAIL GRP | WHOLESALE : NEXT SEASON

{ PRICE GRP | RETAIL : CURRENT + FULL $
WHOLESALE : CURRENT + no $ } UTILIZE

remove cost field ?

assign costs in Product Admin (can also be imported via flat file)

Price Groups

While Availability Groups allow you to offer select products only to certain customers, **Price Groups** allow you to offer the same products to all customers, but at different prices.

A price within a Price Group can be the retail price, a fixed discounted price (such as $5.00), a percentage off from the actual store price (such as 10% off), or a markup from the product cost.

Price Groups can be offered to different customers for different reasons, including:

Wholesale—you might offer products to resellers, such as other online (or offline) retailers, or people with Web sites and storefronts who also want to offer your product(s).

Select Customer Program—you might offer your best customers a fixed price on certain items, or a percentage off one or many products.

Rewards for Creating Customer Accounts—you could tell all customers that if they create a Customer Account, they will be offered discounts.

Members-Only Program—you might offer members of a club a percentage off products in the store.

There is something to keep in mind, however.
While it's possible to assign customers to many price groups (and allow them to purchase at the lowest price possible), and it's possible to create many groups with various discount percentages, there's only one cost (wholesale, or other assigned discount cost) that can be applied to any product. This is the amount you entered (or will enter) in the Cost field in the actual product create/edit screen. (*Chapter Four: Creating Products*)

> **REMEMBER?**
> When creating products, you are prompted to enter the Product Price (the retail price shown in the store), and the Product Cost (usually a wholesale rate).

In other words, you can have a dozen Price Groups, all offering various percentages of discounts. But any Price Group which offers the Cost field will carry the same cost as any of the other groups.

It is also possible to use Price Groups in conjunction with Availability Groups. For example, you might offer members of a club access to all the exclusive products, but members of different levels might have different pricing. Thus, one member might be assigned to one Price Group, and another may be assigned to another Price Group, yet both members may be assigned to the same Availability Group which houses those products.

Types of Pricing

Before creating a Price Group, we need to analyze the various types of costs involved.

Retail – the retail price of the product, which is the price all customers (any of those not assigned to a price group) see by default in the store

Cost – either the wholesale rate you are offering, or another fixed price you will offer to certain customers

Discount From Retail – a percentage off the Retail price

Markup From Cost – a percentage added to the product Cost

It is up to you (or your pricing staff) to determine which way you will offer your Price Groups to your selected customers for that group.

The Percentage Issue

It's possible you are not able to offer the same percentage discount on all products. This usually calls for creating (and assigning customers to) more than one price group. Miva Merchant can handle several price groups, and customers can be assigned to none, some, or all of them.

For example, if you sell new toys and can only offer 10% off Pokemon cards, but want to offer 15% off the new Lego sets, then you would create two Price Groups (one for 10% and one for 15%) and then assign the appropriate products to each one.

Percentages do not have to be whole numbers (1%, 2%). You can enter a fraction of a percent (.25%, .50%), or a combination percentage (1.5%, 4.7%).

 If you plan to offer percentages spontaneously (not regularly) to specific groups of people, or if you want to offer short-term discounts without requiring a customer account, you might want to consider purchasing a third-party coupon module, where users enter a coupon code that applies a discount to specific products ordered.

The Cost Issue

When you created your products, you were shown a Cost field. You can use this field for discount pricing if you wish. It's totally up to you. Just because the field is labeled cost does not mean you cannot use it for other pricing factors.

Creating a Price Group

Once you've figured how you are going to offer the discount, you can add the Price Group to your store.

STEP BY STEP

---

1. In the Admin Menu, click the ► next to **Price Groups**.

2. Click the **Add Price Group** link.

```
┌─────────────────────────────────────────────┐
│ Add Price Group                          [i] │
│                                               │
│ Price Group                                   │
│ Price Group Name: │Members-Standard        │  │
│ Pricing:          ○ Retail                    │
│                   ○ Cost                       │
│                   ● Discount From Retail:│10.00│ % │
│                   ○ Markup From Cost:  │0.00 │ % │
│                                               │
│                              [Add]  [Reset]   │
└─────────────────────────────────────────────┘
```

3. Enter a **Name** for this Price Group. Your customers will not see this name.

4. Select the **Pricing** method. If a percentage, add it as a number with no % sign.

5. Click the **Add** button.

Editing Price Groups

After you've created a Price Group, you will automatically be taken to the **Edit Price Group** screen, where you can begin assigning customers and products. If you need to edit an existing group, click on the ▶ next to **Price Groups**, then click the link of the Price Group you want to edit.

In the **Edit Price Group** screen, you can make changes to the Pricing method for this group the same way you defined the discount method when you created the group.

Customer Assignments to Price Groups

```
┌─────────────────────────────────────────────┐
│ STEP BY STEP                                 │
└─────────────────────────────────────────────┘
```

1. In the Edit Price Group screen, click the **Customers** link.

2. The same way you did for an **Availability Group**, check off all the customers you want to assign to this group.

3. Click the **Update** button.

> If editing an existing group, you can click the Assigned button to remove any customers, or the Unassigned button to add customers who are not yet assigned to the group.

Product Assignments to Price Groups

Just as with Availability Groups, you need to assign products to your Price Group. You can decide to offer discounts on all products or just a few products.

```
┌─────────────────────────────────────────────┐
│ STEP BY STEP                                 │
└─────────────────────────────────────────────┘
```

1. Click the **Products** link.

2. Check off all products you want to assign to this group.

3. Click the **Update** button.

> If editing an existing group, you can click the Assigned button to remove any products, or the Unassigned button to add products that are not yet assigned to the group.

 To add all products at once, choose to view more than 10 per page, then use the + button in the Assigned column to select them all at once.

Deleting Price Groups

Deleting a Price Group will have no effect on the actual products, categories or customers in the store. The only change will be that none of them will be associated with this particular group, because it will no longer exist.

STEP BY STEP
---

1. In the admin menu, click the ▶ next to **Price Groups**.

2. Click on the name of the price group you want to delete.

3. Click the **Delete** button.

Giving Customers the Best Price

Since customers can be assigned to one or more Price Groups, you need to tell Miva Merchant which price they should see and pay. There is no staggering factor here – they either see the highest price or the lowest price. Chances are if you are offering special discounts, this will be the lowest price.

When we created the store, we were given an option for **Price Group Overlap Resolution**. Now's the time to check to make sure we'll be offering the proper price for the customers in conjunction with any Price Groups we've created.

STEP BY STEP
---

1. In the Admin Menu, click on the **link** for you store.

2. Click on the **Settings** link.

3. In the **Price Group Overlap Resolution** menu, choose Highest Price or Lowest Price. Choose the Highest, and the customers will pay the highest possible price. Choose Lowest and the customers will pay the lowest possible price according to any Price Groups to which they may be assigned.

4. Click the **Update** button.

Upsold Products

Pretend you run a music store. Let's say you want to offer Garth Brook's *Chase* CD at just $10.00 to any customer ordering $50 or more worth of product. Or, maybe you have a special sampler CD to offer free with any purchase. Either of these could be an **Upsold Product**.

An upsold product must be an existing product in the store, which is normally regular price. However, if a customer spends a certain amount of money in the store, he or she can be offered the product at a discount.

Upsells are offered during the checkout process after the customer has provided his/her billing and shipping information. It's similar to the teaser aisle in a grocery store.

Adding an Upsold Product

STEP BY STEP

1. In the Admin Menu, click the ▶ next to **Upsale**.

2. Click on the **Add Upsold Product** link.

3. If you know the product code of the item you want to offer, you can enter it in the **Product Code** input box. You can also click the 🔍 button to launch a searchable product listing and, once you find the product you want to upsell, click the 📋 button to select the product.

4. If applicable, enter the **Threshold Percentage of Order Total**, or you can opt to set an **Absolute Price** or set a **Percentage of Original Price**.

Threshold Percentage of Order Total

This percentage is based on the sale price of the product you plan to offer. For example, if the product's regular price is $20 and you want to offer it at half price only if a customer spends $100 or more, then the threshold is 10%.

▶ The product costs $20 regular, the total order amount must be $100, and $10 is 10% of $100.

To calculate the threshold percentage, we use a simple formula, wherein the upsell price of the product is divided by the total amount the order must be for the offer to be made. For example:

Original Price: $30
Upsell Sale Price: $15
Order Must Be: $120
15/20=.125 or, 12.5%

 In Miva Merchants 4.23 and lower, you cannot require a minimum purchase amount to offer an item for free. The item can only be offered for free with any purchase.

Pricing

You can price the upsold item two different ways. You can offer a percentage off the original price, or set an absolute price. In other words, you can set a 20% discount off the original price, or set an actual dollar amount to the product, even $0.00.

5. Click the **Add** button to save the information.

When a shopper goes to checkout, if he or she has met the dollar amount you have set in order to get this item (at a discount), he or she will be asked to accept or reject the special offer. If the item is selected, it is placed in the shopping basket and added to the order. If it is not selected, the shopper will continue checking out as usual.

```
 Select Store  Store Front  Account  Search  Product List  Basket Contents  Checkout

Special Offer: Garth Brooks: Chase
Save $4.99
Offer valid for this order only

Code: GB_Chase
Regular Price: $14.99
Special Price: $10.00
You Save: $4.99
Shipping Weight: 0.40 pounds




       Add One To Order            Do Not Add To Order
```

Many successful stores use upsold items, and some find that giving away something free with each purchase can actually entice visitors to buy something, anything, in order to get something for free.

Examples of Upsale Items

If you are a bit confused about how upsale items work, you are not alone. It's a term many department stores have used for years. So do food chains—ever been asked, "Would you like fries with that?" The difference is, the Upsell feature in Miva Merchant is designed to make those last minute offers to be purchased at a discount.

If you want to offer items based on what the customer is already purchasing, you have to figure the right method for Miva Merchant to use in order to know when to offer the item, and when not to.

Let's say you sell homemade candy in your online store. Chances are your profit level is better than if you were selling in a physical store. So, you decide to offer your sample package of 20 assorted gourmet hard candies for just $1 with every purchase of $20 or more. The packet usually sells for $4.

When a customer has a subtotal of $20 or more, he/she will be offered the item, right? Yes, if it's configured correctly. Remember, the calculation is based on the sale price, not the original price. Thus, the calculation is:

1 divided by 20, which is .05, which translates to 5%

In a fictitious store, you can get the New Jersey's Rockin' Tee for half price when you purchase $10 or more. The Tee normally sells for $16. Here's how we figure the Upsale properties.

Upsold Product		
Product Code:	NJTEE	
Threshold Percentage of Order Total:	80	%
Pricing:	○ Absolute Price:	0.00
	● Percent of Original Price: 50	%

The Tee sells for $16 and we're offering it at HALF PRICE with a purchase of $10 or more. That's 50% off (Percent of Original). Or, we could have just put $8 in the Absolute Price.

The Tee's upsell sale price of $8 is divided by the required purchase price of $10, which equals 80% (which is the Threshold).

Requiring Additional Products

Let's say we've got another T-shirt from the Texas Jam that also costs $16. This Tee can be purchased for just $5 if you spend $20 on any COUNTRY MUSIC selections. This means after creating the upsale, we have to assign specific products that must be purchased in order for the offer to be made.

After adding our Upsale (using absolute cost rather than percentage), we click the **Required Products** link, and choose from the list – everything country, that is.

Upsold Product	**Required Products**			
All Unassigned Assigned			Search:	
Assigned ✓₊ ✓₋	Code	Name		
☑	GB_DoubleLive	Garth Brooks: Double Live		
☑	GB_Chase	Garth Brooks: Chase		

Then we click the **Update** button, and voila! Any customer purchasing $20 or more of country music will now be alerted to take advantage of this special offer.

 Checking off required products does not mean the customer needs to purchase all of those items—only one of the items is required to be in the basket for the upsell product to be offered.

 When using upsale items, you may still want to hype the special offer elsewhere and throughout your site.

Deleting an Upsale

To delete an upsold item, in the Admin Menu, click the Upsale link, check off the **Remove** box, and click the Update button. Only the special offer will be removed; any products assigned will remain in the store's database.

Modifying the Upsale Display

You can opt to display one or many offers during checkout. You can also give the customer the ability to accept only one, or many of the offers.

Why would I offer more than one item?

If you sell products that have many possible add-ons, you may want to offer three options. You may restrict the customer to get only one of the items at a discount, or allow the customer to purchase them all if he/she so desires.

When offering more than one Upsale in an order, the customer will be presented with a list. The customer checks off any items he/she would like to add to the order.

Special Offers:
Offers valid for this order only
You may select one or more of the following:

Add to Basket	Code	Product	Regularly	Special	Save
☐	GB_DoubleLive	Garth Brooks: Double Live	$24.99	$19.99	$5.00
☐	GB_Chase	Garth Brooks: Chase	$14.99	$10.00	$4.99

STEP BY STEP

1. In the Admin Menu, click the **Upsale** link.

2. Click the **Settings** link.

3. Enter the maximum number of offers to make, and the maximum number of offers the customer can select.

Upsale

Upsold Products Settings

Upsold Products to Show: 3
Max Number of Upsold Products to Select: 3

Upsale updated

4. Click the **Update** button.

When you have created more Upsales than can possibly be offered for any particular order, the offers will be made automatically and sometimes randomly. For example, if there are 15 possible special offers for the customer's current order, and you've told Miva Merchant to only offer a maximum of three items, the customer may see three completely different items than another customer.

Viewing Upsales in the Edit Product Screen

You can view *required* Upsale features from product screens in the Admin Area.

STEP BY STEP

    1. In the Admin Menu, click the **Products** link.

    2. Search for the product that is a required product purchase for an upsale and click the 🖻 button.

    3. Click the **Upsold Products** link.

    4. View the product(s) that will be offered as upsales when this particular product is purchased. If none are listed, then this product is not required in order to be offered another item.

Running an Affiliate Program

An affiliate program allows your store to get referrals from other sites, while only paying for the advertising if sales or visits are made. Other people post your ad on their site, and when visitors click on it, they are taken to your store. You can opt to pay the affiliate based on the number of visitors, or a percentage of sales that are made.

Miva Merchant has a basic affiliate program built in versions 4.x and higher. There are also third-party solutions that provide more extensive features.

 Before enacting any affiliate program you should first research local laws and define your legal terms to which you expect affiliates to agree. It is also wise to have an attorney look over the terms before they are posted.

Configuring the Affiliate Program

In order to take on affiliates, you must first enact the program included in Miva Merchant versions 4.x and up.

STEP BY STEP

1. In the Admin Menu, click the **Affiliate Configuration** link.

2. Set the Options for the program.

> **Affiliate Configuration**
>
> **Options**   Lost Password Email Affiliates Affiliate Email Notification Payouts
> MMUI Header & Footer MMUI Affiliate Login
>
> ☑ Activate Affiliate Program
> Default Application Status: Pending ▾
> Default Commission Per Referral (hit):   0.0000
> Default Commission Percent of Order: 10.00   Subtotal ▾
> Default Commission Flat Fee Per Order: 0.00
> Payout Threshold: 25.00
> Link Image: ⚬
> Link Text:
> Terms:
>
> Update   Reset

Activate Affiliate Program – must be checked for this feature to work.

Default Application Status – it is recommended that all signups are **Pending** until you can approve or reject them.

Default Commission Per Referral (hit) – the amount you will pay for each time a visitor comes to your store after clicking on the affiliate's link. Many programs do not offer a pay-per-hit because anyone can continuously click the affiliate's link to add up. Enter this is a whole number with no currency symbols.

Default Commission Percent of Order – enter the percent of the total order you are willing to pay. This can be 5%, 10% or whatever you like. Enter this is a whole number, such as 5.00 for 5%.

Default Commission Flat Fee Per Order – you can optionally offer affiliates a certain dollar amount per order, such as $.50 or $1.00. You can also choose to calculate the commission against either the orders subtotal (price of products, less tax and shipping) or the order total, which includes shipping and tax if they are present in the order. You probably want to calculate against just the subtotal.

Payout Threshold – this is the dollar amount the affiliate's earnings must reach before they can be paid.

Link Image – the image the affiliate is to place on his/her site. This usually follows the format of a banner ad.

Link Text – the text link the affiliate must display on his/her site.

Terms – outline in great detail the terms of your affiliate program.

3. Click the **Update** button.

4. Click the **Lost Password Email** link.

5. Enter the email address the lost password email will be sent FROM (and include a CC if you want someone other than the affiliate to receive it). Also enter the **Subject** and **Header Text** (which will precede the password information).

6. Click the **Update** button.

7. Click the **Affiliate Email Notification** Link.

8. Set the parameters, telling Miva Merchant where to send the New Message from and to (or uncheck the Message box to not send one). Enter the Subject and text for the email.

9. Click the **Header & Footer** link.

Here, you can create headers and footers for various screens. They are:

Affiliate Login—the screen where affiliates log in to check their stats and get their link.

Create Affiliate Account—the screen where potential affiliates enter information to apply to be an affiliate.

Edit Affiliate Account—the screen where existing affiliates edit information, such as their mailing address.

10. Click the **Affiliate Login Link** link.

Here you can set options for displaying an affiliate link in your store. By default, this link will appear at the top of the category tree, below the Customer Sign In link (if activated).

Recommendation:
Most successful online stores put the affiliate link in the footer of the entire site. This can be done with a simple HTML link later.

11. Click the **Update** button.

Adding Affiliates

You can manually add affiliates to the affiliate program. Or, you can wait for them to signup.

STEP BY STEP

1. In the Affiliate Configuration screen, click the **Affiliates** link.

2. Click the button to create a new affiliate.

3. Enter a unique login, email address, and password for the new affiliate. Remember, codes cannot contain spaces nor special characters.

4. Select whether the affiliate is approved, rejected, or in a pending status.

5. Click the **Info** link.

6. Enter all information, including site name and URL, mailing address, etc.

7. Click the **Commission** link.

8. You can override the default program settings, so each affiliate can earn money by different methods or amounts. Make any changes on the commissions for this affiliate here. If you want the default settings to apply to this affiliate, do nothing.

9. Click the **Add** button.

Editing & Managing Affiliates

You can change an affiliate's status, information and/or commissions at any time.

If you set all new affiliates as a Pending status, you will need to visit your Admin Area to approve or reject affiliates.

STEP BY STEP

1. In the Affiliate Configuration screen, click the **Affiliates** link.

2. Find the affiliate you want to modify and click the 🗐 button.

3. Verify the status of the affiliate – if it is Pending, you want to approve or reject the affiliate. Rejecting an affiliate will not remove the affiliate applicant's record from your store.

4. If needed, click the **Info** or **Commission** links to change affiliate information. Be sure to click the **Update** button if you make changes.

5. Click the **Earnings** link.

You can remove or void any commissions earned. For example, if an order was canceled, you may want to remove the listing. Or, if you find the affiliate is cheating the program, you may want to void the payout.

To void an earning, click the 🗐 button next to that actual earning, and make the adjustments, as outlined in the next section.

6. When finished, click the **Update** button.

Voiding Specific Affiliate Earnings

You can avoid earnings on any order placed via an affiliate. This feature is designed to be used a customer cancels an order, or if you find there was an error or terms violation.

STEP BY STEP

1. In the Affiliate Configuration screen, click the **Affiliates** link.

2. Find the affiliate and open the record for editing, then click the **Earnings** link.

3. Next to the order to void the earnings for, click the 🖳 button.

4. Check the **Void** box.

5. Enter the **Void Reason** so you have a record.

6. Click the **Add** button.

 The Voided By field will always be completed according to the user who is logged into the admin.

Adding & Adjusting Affiliate Earnings

You can give affiliates credit for sales that did not go through their defined affiliate link. For example, if a customer orders, then tells you they were referred by one of your affiliates, you may want to give that affiliate credit for the sale anyway.

You can also void using the following method. We suggest you void earnings using the previous method as you will be less prone to making mistakes.

STEP BY STEP

1. In the Affiliate Configuration screen, click the **Affiliates** link.

2. Find the affiliate and open the record for editing, then click the Earnings link.

3. In the very top right corner, click the 🗅 button.

4. Enter the **Order Number**, **Order Amount** and the amount **Earned** by the affiliate.

5. Enter an **Adjustment Reason**, so you will have a record.

6. Click the **Add** button.

Logging Affiliate Payouts

You'll want to log your payouts you make so you can verify what is owed. Affiliates can also log in to their affiliate account and see payment records.

 The following requires that you have affiliate sales logged in your store. You may want to place some test orders—or create some earnings adjustments—with a test affiliate account to see how this works.

STEP BY STEP

---

1. In the Affiliate Configuration screen, click the **Payouts** link.

2. In the top right-hand corner, click the 🔲 button.

3. Click the **Continue** button.

4. A screen will display, showing you which affiliates are to be paid, along with the amount to pay.

Add Payout	
Payout Threshold: 25.00	
Payee Count: 1	
Payout Amount: 28.08	
Continue	Reset

5. Click the **Payout** link.

6. Once you have cut the check(s), you can check off the **Processed** box, noting that the affiliate has been paid.

7. Click the **Update** button.

After processing payouts, there will be a new entry under each affiliate's Earnings section.

Logging Individual Payouts

You can log and process a payout for a specific affiliate without handling payouts for any other affiliate.

To log a payout for a single affiliate, open the affiliate's record for editing, and click the **Commission** link. Next, click the **Payout (This Affiliate Only)** link, then the **Payout** link at the top of the screen. Mark payout as processed, then click **Update**.

Troubleshooting the Affiliate Program

Existing Customers Don't Qualify

In earlier versions of Miva Merchant, the affiliate program runs off cookies. Therefore, if a customer has previously shopped your store from the same computer he/she is using now, no affiliate credits will be given. For example, if Tom shopped your store from his home PC last week, and this week shops from the same computer, but instead clicks on Joe's affiliate link, Joe will not get credit for the sale.

This issue was fixed in future versions. If you run into this problem follow the steps for making affiliate earning adjustments to give the affiliate credit for the order.

Chapter Seven

Order Processing

Miva Merchant's job is to allow online shoppers to place orders. Though Miva Merchant is not a complete order processing package, there are some features which assist in the processing of online orders.

If you setup the Merchant Notification feature (*Chapter Four: Adding the Main Store*), then either you (or the order processor of the store) will receive an e-mail whenever an order is placed. In fact, an entire list of people can receive copies of every order.

While an attractive and easy to navigate store will bring potential customers in, it is timely order processing (and product quality, of course) that will keep them returning, as well as referring your store to others. You can have the best-looking, fastest loading store, and the best quality products, but if your customers can't receive their orders in a timely fashion, forget about it.

Remember the holiday season of 1999? Two high-profile, multi-billion dollar stores were boycotted by online shoppers because presents couldn't be delivered on time. Some customers didn't receive orders until mid-January. The result? Both of these online moguls lost thousands of customers. One felt so bad they gave $100 gift certificates to all those affected by their lack of ability to do the one thing customers wanted – timely shipments. Is this something you can afford?

E-commerce Tip...
Use good packaging, a responsible shipping method, and have a plan for action when multiple orders arrive. Timely delivery can make or break any online business.

In fact, many customers are willing to pay a little more if they know they will receive their item(s) in one piece and within a week. Keep this in mind – it is another issue that can make or break an online venture.

IMPORTANT:
In order to be able to view and process orders right now, you will need to place some test orders in your store.

Take a few minutes to place some test orders, and be sure to jot down (but not dwell on) things that irk you, or need improvement. You will address these later.

Viewing & Editing Orders

With Miva Merchant you can work with orders one at a time, or work with a batch of orders (a group of all recent orders).

✓ *Miva Merchant is not an order processing program. Thus, it doesn't give you all the core features of software programs designed to handle returns, exchanges, post-order discounts, etc. There are several third-party solutions (modules and standalone software) available to give you full order processing capabilities.*

Working with Single Orders

Working with single orders takes a significant amount of time. However, if you only get a few orders each day, and want to print invoices as each comes in, you may opt to work with orders right through the order information screen in the Admin area.

STEP BY STEP
---

1. In the Admin Menu, click the ▶ next to **Order Processing**.

2. Click the ▶ next to **Un-batched** Orders.

3. Click the link for the order you want to view.

You can correct the customer's billing and shipping addresses.

Information about the order is separated into three screens. Initially the **Customer Information** screen appears, displaying all of the contact information for billing and shipping.

4. Make any necessary changes, then click **Update**. If no changes are needed, move to the next step.

5. Click the Order Information link. This area lists the item(s) ordered, the price paid for each, the sales tax, shipping charge and total amount. Any attributes will also be listed, along with any additional charges. Here, only the tax, shipping and total can be adjusted.

Edit Order: #100000

Customer Information   **Order Information**   Check Payment

Code	Product	Quantity	Price/Ea.	Total
GB_Chase	Garth Brooks: Chase	1	14.99	14.99
GB_DoubleLive	Garth Brooks: Double Live	1	24.99	24.99
TEE_Vneck	V-Neck 100% Cotten Tee	1	12.00	12.00
	SIZE: XXL		2.00	2.00
	COLOR: RED			

Shipping: Free Shipping: 0.00
Sales Tax: 0.00
Total: 53.98

Update   Delete   Reset

While you may update the shipping, sales tax and order total, you may not make changes to pricing and cannot add any line items (products or discounts).

Editing order totals will not affect the total amount processed via a payment gateway.

6. Click the **Payment** link.

7. The customer's payment details are what you need to get payment for the order. In this example, the customer has decided to pay by check (which will be mailed to us).

   When credit card orders are placed, this screen will display the credit card number (unless it is encrypted or not stored), the expiration date and name on the card. Some merchant gateways will not display this in detail, so what appears is dependent upon the payment method and any configurations.

8. If you made any changes, click the **Update** button. Otherwise, click the **Reset** button.

Printing Single Orders

You can print single invoices on a per-order basis right from the customer's order screen.

Just click on the 🖨 button in the top right corner or the **Customer Information** screen.

Deleting Single Orders

The only time you should delete orders in the editable screens is if the orders is a test or if it is a failed order. You should be keeping records of all your actual sales, even if they are later canceled.

STEP BY STEP

1. Click the ▶ next to **Order Processing**.

2. Click the ▶ next to **Un-batched Orders**.

3. Click the order you want to delete.

4. Click the **Delete** button.

The printer button is not always printer-friendly, as orders are rendered in HTML. Browsers vary, so results may not be the same for all users.

Batch Processing – The Right Way to Process

When orders are grouped according to the date they were submitted, you can better track them and look them up. In Miva Merchant, a group of orders is called a **Batch**.

Essentially, you should batch orders regularly, and name the batch using a logical method so you can quickly locate orders in the future.

As you can see by the example to your right, batching orders makes it easier for one to find what orders were purchased during a particular timeframe.

Batching serves other purposes as well:

> ▼ Order Processing
> • Create Batch
> ▶ 06/02/2003: 3435
> ▶ 06/27/2003: 3492
> ▶ 06/30/2003: 3498
> ▶ 07/02/2003: 3506
> ▶ 07/02/2003: 3511
> ▶ 07/04/2003: 3515
> ▶ 07/05/2003: 3519
> ▶ 07/06/2003: 3525
> ▶ 07/09/2003: 3564

Reports – you can run printed reports of all orders in a batch, which can then be filed, or noted for processing.

Processing – if you are using a module for a third-party payment system, such as CyberSource Payment Services or CyberCash, this feature will actually mark for payment the orders in the batch.

New Orders – any unbatched orders will sit loose at the bottom of the list, so you'll know which orders have been worked on, and which ones haven't.

Exporting Orders – Miva Merchant includes an order export utility for tracking sales which will only export batched orders. We'll discuss this procedure later.

Our Recommendation

Batch your orders each time you process them. If you don't you'll find yourself filing through a long list of orders, not knowing which have been tended to and which haven't, and you'll have to manually track all your online orders in order to compare them with the actual completed sales.

Orders don't necessarily have to be batched every single day. It all depends on when you plan to charge and ship your orders.

Batching Orders

STEP BY STEP

1. In the Admin Menu, click the ▶ next to **Order Processing**.

2. Click the **Create Batch** link.

3. Enter a name for the batch. We recommend naming the batch the last order number that will be in the batch. Miva Merchant will already show the date of the batch; using the last order number may make it easier for you to locate old orders.

   > Create Batch: 1 new order
   >
   > Batch Name: 12967
   >
   > Create   Reset

4. Click the **Create** button.

Running Batch Reports

Immediately after you create a batch, you will be prompted to run a report. This is not necessary, and you can always run the report later so long as you don't delete the batch.

The batch report is a printable report that contains each order in the batch.

STEP BY STEP

1. In the Admin Menu, click the ▶ next to **Order Processing**.

2. Click the ▶ next to the batch for which you want to run a report.

3. Click the **Run Report** link.

4. In the right-hand screen, use the pull-down menu to select Standard Batch Report.

    Unless third-party batch and/or invoice modules are installed, only one type of report is available: Standard Batch Report.

5. Click the **Run Report** button.

We do not recommend using the standard batch report included with Miva Merchant as a customer invoice or receipt. Depending on the configuration of any credit card payment modules, complete credit card information may appear on the report. Also, the report does not contain your company information.

Printing Batch Reports

When you select to run the batch report, your orders will appear in a screen like this:

Standard Batch Report

Order #100000

Ship To:		Bill To:	
Name:	Test Order	Name:	Test Order
Email Address:	author@mvcommerce.net	Email Address:	author@mvcommerce.net
Phone Number:	305-752-3943	Phone Number:	305-752-3943
Fax Number:		Fax Number:	
Company:		Company:	
Address:	P O Box 827	Address:	P O Box 827
	Clifton Park, NY 12065		Clifton Park, NY 12065
	US		US

Shipping Information:	Payment Information:
Shipping Method: Free Shipping	**Check**
	Check #: 111

Code	Product	Quantity	Price/Ea.	Total
GB_Chase	Garth Brooks: Chase	1	$14.99	$14.99
GB_DoubleLive	Garth Brooks: Double Live	1	$24.99	$24.99
TEE_Vneck	V-Neck 100% Cotten Tee	1	$12.00	$12.00
	SIZE: XXL		$2.00	$2.00
	COLOR: RED			
		Shipping: Free Shipping:		$0.00
		Sales Tax:		$0.00
		Total: $53.98		

To print the report, use your browser's print command.

 Miva Merchant's Standard Batch Report runs orders together, which means an order may print on the bottom half on one page with the rest printing on the top half on the next page. There are two ways to force orders to print one per page.

After running the report in the Admin, use the mouse to highlight each individual order (on a PC, hold the left mouse button down at the top of the order, and drag until you reach the end of that one order). Then click on File... Print... and choose to print only the selection.

Purchase a third-party module that runs the reports one order per printed page.

Processing Batched Orders

When you batch orders, you are filing them together according to when the orders were placed.

If you are utilizing a third-party payment gateway system that supports Miva Merchant's built-in processing function (used only when orders are authorized in real time), then the following steps must be taken in order for you to get paid. This is how you tell the gateway that you are filling the order.

 In order to process orders this way, you must batch the orders first.

A payment gateway is a company that approves credit card charges in real-time; an order cannot be completed to the customer if the credit card is declined. This service is used in conjunction with a credit card merchant account and incurs its own separate fees. If your gateway doesn't require processing through Miva Merchant, or if you will approve credit card payments manually, then the following exercise won't do much for you. Essentially, it will show that the order has been filled, but no funds will actually be transferred.

If you are not using a gateway that requires processing, you can skip this step of order processing.

STEP BY STEP

1. In the Admin menu, click the ▶ next to **Order Processing**.

2. Click the ▶ next to the batch you want to process.

3. Click the **Process Orders** link.

4. Check off the orders you want to **Process** or **Mark As Processed**. If supported, be sure you follow the proper method as outlined by your merchant account gateway.

5. Click the **Process** (when using a gateway that supports it) or **Mark As Processed** button as necessary.

Once an order is processed or marked as processed, it will no longer be available in this listing.

Some prior versions of Miva Merchant provide for each order to be processed separately.

Deleting Batched Orders

When all orders in a batch are complete, you may wish to delete the batch. There are several reasons people choose to delete batches, including:

You should always backup orders before deleting them.
Be sure to review the next section before removing any "real" orders.

♦ **To remove sensitive information.** If you are using simple validation for credit cards, or have opted to keep a copy of credit card numbers with the order, then any orders or batches that remain on the server also keep that information there. This means anyone with access to your server has access to that payment information. We've yet to run across a merchant account provider who allows the data to be stored on the server.

♦ If you run an active store, the databases storing this information can get large in size.

♦ Keeping it clean makes running the store easier.

However, if you are using a third-party customer order tracking module, you may need to leave these batches on the server. Check with the developer to see what is required.

 If you are using a payment gateway which requires processing via the Miva Merchant Admin, make sure you process all orders in the batch before deleting.

To delete a batch, just click the ▶ next to the name of the batch, and click the **Delete Batch** button.

After deleting batches, the store's data files need to be packed. See *Chapter Eight: Store Maintenance* for more information.

Backing Up / Exporting Orders

No ifs, ands or buts...you should backup every order on the server for record-keeping, tax purposes and analyzing sales over a period of time. **Orders need to be batched before they are backed up using the admin utility, and you should always backup the orders before deleting a batch.**

You also may need to export orders so you can import them into third-party order processing software.

Information about orders is stored in a few backend database files. In order to back these up via the Miva Merchant Admin Area, you have to export the batches to a **flat file**.

A flat file is a generic text file which can be converted to a spreadsheet or database program, such as Microsoft Excel or Microsoft Access. You can then manipulate the data and use it for various purposes. Refer to the manual or other instructions for your software on charting this data.

Some 4.x versions of Miva Merchant also include an export module for QuickBooks.

Exporting Processed Orders to a Flat File (.dat)

Exporting orders to a flat file is a simple process. Retrieving the data file requires an FTP or remote connection to the server. You may need to check with your host for the available options.

Remember—only batched orders can be exported this way. All orders you back up should already be processed (completed). **The exported orders file will not include the credit card data.**

STEP BY STEP

1. In the Admin Menu, click the ▶ next to the store's **Utilities** link. (This is the first occurrence of the word "utilities," as there is another section named the same for the mall.)

2. Click the ▶ next to **Export Data**.

3. Click the **Export Orders To Flat File** link.

You need to select the batch to export, the name of the file you want created (or data appended to), what delimiter you want used (if necessary, refer to documentation on the software you plan to use to view the data), and whether or not you want to replace any current data already in the export file on the server.

4. In the **Batch to Export** pull-down menu, select the batch you want to export.

5. If you want, enter a different name for the export file. By default, the file name will be orders.dat.

6. Choose the delimiter.

> By default, the orders.dat file (the default file name for exported orders) is tab-delimited. This means the text file will contain a TAB SPACE between each field in the orders records. Tab-delimited files can usually be opened by any common spreadsheet or database program. However, if you know what you are doing, you can tell Miva Merchant to use a different delimiter, such as a comma or the pipe character.

7. Choose whether you want to replace any existing data or if you want to append the batch to existing data.

> By default, each exported batch will append to the existing orders.dat file. This means any orders you export next week will automatically be added to the existing file, which includes orders exported today. If you choose Replace File, then any previous exports to this specific file will be overwritten.

8. Click the **Export** button.

9. Repeat steps 4-5 for each subsequent batch you'd like to export that is listed in the pull-down menu.

Should I append or replace data?

Let's say you want to export orders on a weekly basis and import them into Microsoft Excel for analysis. On week one, you export batches for days 1-7, choosing to append the data to the orders.dat file.

The next week, since you've already imported the information into the first spreadsheet, you export days 8-14, and choose Replace file, since you only need the information for these particular days (the others are already in the offline spreadsheet).

In this case, each week when you export, you will choose Replace file for the first batch listed, and Append for each thereafter until all seven days are exported.

Now let's say you want to export orders every week, but you want to keep a different .dat file for each on the server. In this case, you would enter a different file name for the exported orders.

Either way you choose, you are able to export each week, even when you batch each day, and import your data into Excel for analysis.

Once your exports are tested to be intact, you can then delete the batches you exported, as you now have a backup of those orders.

Retrieving Flat File Exported Orders

After exporting your orders, you'll want to get the **orders.dat** (or other file, if you changed the name) off the server and onto your computer.

The orders.dat file is located in the data directory on the server, and you will need to FTP or similar access to the server to get this file. For some, this file is located in the **mivadata** or **htsdata** folder off the web-accessed root of the server. This folder is supposed to be located outside the Merchant folder on root of your server (if it's not, contact your ISP).

Inside that data directory, you will need to navigate to the Merchant/0000000x/export directory. There you'll find the file (orders.dat).

Once you've found the file, you can download it to your computer (in ASCII mode), then import it into a spreadsheet or database program.

Whether or not the orders.dat file is in the mivadata (or htsdata) directory, if you cannot access one of these folders on your server, you should contact your ISP – some restrict you from accessing folders on the root of the absolute server. This means no one, not even a developer, could help repair any database files that might be damaged if you make a serious mistake.

Exporting Orders in QuickBooks Format

Only batched orders can be exported to a file that is importable by QuickBooks. As with any other batched orders, all orders you back up should already be processed (completed).

 The QuickBooks Export module was removed in Miva Merchant version 4.21. Miva Synchro was developed to synch data with QuickBooks. See Chapter Twelve: Store Add-Ons.

STEP BY STEP

1. In the Admin Menu, click the ▶ next to the store's **Utilities** link. (This is the first occurrence of the word "utilities," as there is another section named the same for the mall.)

2. Click the ▶ next to **Export Data**.

3. Click the **QuickBooks Export** link.

4. If you're new to QuickBooks, you should accept the default filename of **quickbatch.iif**.

5. If you have previously exported and want to append this data to the existing file, then choose **Append To File**. Otherwise, choose **Replace File** to overwrite old data that you have already imported into QuickBooks.

6. Click the **Customers** link.

7. Use the checkboxes to select the customer information you want to export to the file.

8. Click the **Orders** link.

9. From the **Batch to Export** list, select which batch you want to export to the file.

10. Click the **Export** button.

After exporting one batch, Miva Merchant will default to the Append to File option and will retain your settings on the Customers screen. Therefore, you can simply click the Batch to Export list, choose your next batch, and click Export again until all batches have been exported.

You will need to connect to the server to obtain the .iif file, just as you would for the orders.dat file.

To import your batches into QuickBooks, follow the instructions for the program.

The QuickBooks module will not export credit card information.

The QuickBooks export module may not work with all versions of QuickBooks.

Chapter Eight

Store Maintenance

Your store will only operate as well as you maintain its information. Now that you have an online store, you want to take every step possible to keep it in tip-top shape.

The information in this chapter is vital for your store's operation. It is also contains some of the most common issues users bring to the attention Miva Merchant developers. Learning these steps can save headaches and money.

This chapter is so important we wish it were simple enough to put on page one. Unfortunately, you need to have learned the process of creating your store in order to understand maintenance procedures.

The best thing you can do is copy this section and tack it to the bulletin board, then live by the necessities.

Taking the Store Offline

From time to time you may want to make updates to your online store without allowing customers to see a work in progress. You may also need to perform other tasks that may require the store be taken offline.

Maintenance Mode allows you to take the store offline for any maintenance or for emergencies, such as data corruption. It also allows you to notify customers when the store will go offline (for scheduled maintenance), and provide any message to them.

STEP BY STEP

1. In the Admin Menu, click **your store's link**.

2. Click the **Maintenance Mode** link.

For scheduled maintenance, you can warn customers in advance. You can even present a custom message.

Store Activity:	⦿ Store Online
	○ Offline At 13:58 On Month: 08 Day: 23 Year: 2004
	It is currently: 13:28:41 EDT on 08/23/2004
No New Customer:	0 Minutes before store goes offline.
Warning Message:	%store_name% will be closing in %maint_countdown% minutes
Maintenance Message:	Sorry, %store_name% is closed for maintenance. We will re-

Available Tokens:	%store_name%	Name of your store
	%maint_countdown%	Minutes until store closes
	%maint_countdown_formatted%	Formatted time until store closes
	%maint_time%	The time your store goes offline
	%maint_date%	The date your store goes offline

3. Set the options.

> **Store Activity** – you can toggle between the store being online or offline. If the store is set to go offline, you can set a predetermined date and time. If it needs to go offline right away, you would enter the current date and time.

> **No New Customer** - allows you to prohibit new shoppers from using the store if they enter X number of minutes before scheduled maintenance

Warning Message - allows you to display a warning message above the navigation bar, telling customers the store will be going offline. You can use the available tokens listed at the bottom of this configuration screen to display information dynamically.

Maintenance Message - allows you to display a message, telling customers the store is offline for maintenance. You can use the available tokens listed at the bottom of this configuration screen to display information dynamically.

4. Click the **Update** button.

When to Take the Store Offline

Of course you need a reason to take the store offline. Here's a few common ones:

◆ When performing mass imports of products or updates of existing products (updating price, etc.).

◆ When manually changing inventory levels on several products (to prevent ordering of those products while you are changing levels).

◆ When issues arise that cause errors in the store.

◆ Whenever you delete expired baskets and pack data (next section).

◆ Whenever you are unable to take orders.

Turning the Store Online

To turn the store back online, click the **Maintenance Mode** link, select **Store Online**, then click the **Update** button.

Delete, Pack, Pack

As potential customers navigate your store, various database files are accessed. Over time and use, like anything else, these files can become filled with more information than is needed.

That's why we regularly:

> **Delete** Expired Shopping Baskets
> **Pack** the Mall's Data Files
> **Pack** the Store's Data Files

Many users might tell you to only perform these functions once in a while. We've noticed that, at least for active stores, making this a daily routine can help cut down potential problems. In fact, the **most common problem reported with stores is corrupt data**, and it is quite often avoidable.

In the Admin Menu, you'll find two **Utilities** directories. The first one shown here is for the STORE you are editing. The bottom one, just above the About Miva Merchant link, is for the MALL. Even though you might only have one store, that store is still considered to be housed in an "invisible" mall that only you know about.

| The first occurrence of the Utilities link is for the store. |

The following tasks are _essential_ to your store's operation. We cannot stress this enough.

These tasks can also cause shopping delays while they are performed. If you plan to perform these tasks during peak times, you should first take the store offline.

Deleting Shopping Baskets

As potential customers move around your site, they are assigned a Session ID number, and if they place items in their basket, they are assigned an order number. If a customer leaves without ordering, that order number sits in a database until it is deleted (and possibly used again). Because of this, you'll notice skips in some of your order numbers. Obviously, not every person who enters your store is going to buy something. Many will place items in the shopping basket, then change their minds and just leave.

For this reason, you want to delete these expired baskets – they time out after 60 minutes. Depending on how active your store is, you may want to delete the expired baskets every day or every week.

✔ *Some Miva Merchant users get nervous when order numbers are skipped. This does not necessarily mean there is a problem. In a perfect environment, every order would have a subsequent order number, but keep in mind that the order number is nothing more than a unique identifier of the customer's order.*

Our Recommendation
You are always better safe than sorry. Perform the tasks of Delete, Pack, Pack daily.

STEP BY STEP

1. In the Admin Menu, click the ► next to your store's link.

2. Click the ► next to **Utilities** (the one for your store, not the mall).

3. Click the **Delete Shopping Baskets** link.

```
┌─────────────────────────────────────────────┐
│ Delete Shopping Baskets:              🌐      │
│ MvCommerce.Net                                │
│                                               │
│ ┌───────────────────────────────────────────┐│
│ │ Delete:  ⊙ Expired                         ││
│ │          ○ All                             ││
│ │ Recover Order Numbers:  ⊙ Yes  ○ No        ││
│ └───────────────────────────────────────────┘│
│ ┌───────────────────────────────────────────┐│
│ │                        Delete │ Cancel      ││
│ └───────────────────────────────────────────┘│
└─────────────────────────────────────────────┘
```

4. Choose to either delete only **Expired** baskets (ones that visitors let time out) or **All** baskets (any basket that hasn't become a completed order—which could be baskets of current existing shoppers. Unless you have a problem and have already taken the store into a scheduled offline maintenance mode, you should only delete the expired baskets.

5. Choose Yes or No on **Recovering Order Numbers**. If you choose yes, any skipped order numbers will be available for assignment on orders. If you choose no, those order numbers will never be used in your store. *We recommend choosing NO in order to minimize potential data corruption.*

6. Click the **Delete** button.

When complete, you should see a message stating that the baskets have been deleted.

Packing the Mall's Data Files

As you delete information from the mall, such as modules or stores, etc., the items are still stored in Miva Merchant, they are just marked for deletion. When you pack the data files, the items are actually removed, freeing up space and avoiding conflicts.

STEP BY STEP

---

1. In the Admin menu, click the ▶ next to the mall's **Utilities** link.

2. Click the **Pack Data Files** link.

When complete, you should see a message stating that the domain data files have been packed.

Packing the Store's Data Files

The store itself is prone to problems because it contains your product information, category information, customer and ordering information, payment information, and a slew of other information, all stored in database files. Many third-party modules also run their own database files, leaving even more possibilities for issues to arise. But you can avoid the common pitfalls by just listening and believing—**packing your store's data is essential**.

Why is packing data so important?

Whenever you add data to your store that is stored in a database file, it is assigned a unique record number. The code, right? Wrong. While codes must be unique, there's a "hidden" record number that is never seen in the Admin Area. It's stored with the database record and is used to cross reference databases (using index records). These record numbers are key, which is why the average Miva Merchant user should never even try to mess with them.

When you delete products, orders, batches, or anything else recorded as a database record from the store, they are only marked for deletion. Only packing the data files will remove them from the database file completely. The reasons for this is a whole other discussion (that we won't be discussing here).

To the Miva Merchant user, the advantage of this process is that *usually* when something is deleted, it is salvageable if the proper steps are taken **before** packing the data. The disadvantage is that failing to pack the data can cause those unique record numbers to be reused—so when you finally do attempt to pack the data, you can't because there are duplicate record numbers.

And the nasty part? Unless you are a database guru, you have to get someone to fix the problem. That someone is usually a Miva Business Partner, and the service isn't free. In short, failing to pack your store's data can cost you a hundred bucks or more. All because you skipped a simple process.

 If you do not pack data after deleting <u>anything</u> in the Admin Area (including orders, products, customers, categories, attributes, etc.) you leave yourself prone to errors and duplicate record numbers.

STEP BY STEP

1. In the Admin Menu, click the ► next to your store.

2. Click the ► next to **Utilities** (the FIRST occurrence under your store).

3. Click the **Pack Data Files** link.

4. When complete, you should see a message stating that the data files have been packed.

 If you receive errors during this process, it is possible you have corrupt files or duplicate order numbers. Contact Miva Corporation or a Certified Miva Business Partner for assistance.

How should I pack my store's data?
Any time you are deleting products, orders, attributes...*anything*...pack the store's data. If it seems like we're hitting you over the head with a hammer, we are. You can never pack enough.

Backing Up Server Files

You should backup the files on your server on a regular basis. If you are familiar with the directories enough so far, you can create a backup folder on your computer, and use an FTP program to backup all the files located in both the Merchant2 folder (or other named Miva Merchant folder), as well as the data files (usually located in the mivadata or htsdata folder).

If you are not yet accustomed to doing this, you should consider paying someone to do it for you. As well, you should make sure your hosting provider backs up all server files on a regular basis; most IHPs do this daily or weekly for their own protection, but don't ever assume this. Stop for a minute right now and call your host. If they are not backing up your site, tell them you want it done. Some may charge for this, but it should not be an outrageous cost.

If my host backs up, why should I?
Ahhh, the question of many…and answered by those who just assumed.

First, you should never rely on one backup source. This is your business, your livelihood, and if it all crashed tomorrow, where would you be? How do you think so many corporations headquartered out of New York City stayed in business, despite equipment loss, after 9-11? Because they weren't relying on their individual terminals as their only means of maintaining information. It doesn't matter how great a facility is housing your server—if it's wiped out due to a hurricane, it's gone, and it will take some time to put that information in another location—a time during which you have no access to the data.

Second, and this is sadly true, some hosts fail to backup their servers as they intend or claim to do. The only way you'll find out about this kind of problem is if you need a backup restored. Why get stuck saying, "If I only knew…"

Third, while most hosts charge a nominal fee for restoring backups, some fees can be quite expensive, especially if it means going to archives on tape.

And, lastly, there's no guarantee that anyone will be in business the following day. If your host were to go belly up, what happens to your site?

We don't mean to scare you, but the scenarios have all happened. Some issues have been fixed quickly, while others have resulted in hefty costs to rebuild entire sites.

And...how much should it cost?
Most hosting plans include the cost of regular backups. Some have additional options for a fee, and some charge according to what you want—daily, weekly or monthly backups. Daily backups usually cost more, but some hosts absorb some of the cost by backing up all the sites on a server together.

Costs also may differ based on the media to which the backup is stored. Some hosts backup to other servers, while others backup to tape. The ideal process is a backup to tape that is then stored in a fireproof vault (some hosts store tapes in safety deposit boxes at their local bank).

For manual backups by a third-party, expect to pay at least a hundred bucks. Reputable companies or individuals will put the data on a CD and provide it to you.

As for backup restores, it all depends on the host or company. We've seen it cost anywhere from $25 to $250, depending on the type of restore.

Chapter Nine

Advanced Store Administration

Now that you've learned the ins and outs of the administration area of Miva Merchant, and what you can do to create and maintain the online store, it's time to move on to some of the advanced implementations, if you so desire.

None of the explanations here are required for the Miva Merchant online store to run, but you'll find that many can assist you when administering the store. Also, you might find some of these a little difficult, especially if you are not technically-inclined. If this is the case, you're not alone. Many new store users find they have to hire someone to implement additional features in Miva Merchant.

Giving Others Admin Permissions

If other people need to be able to perform administrative functions, such as order processing or product administration, then you'll need to give them access to the Admin Area. It is recommended that you do not allow anyone to login with the same username as anyone else. Only one person should have the admin password used to create the store, and that is you. You can offer the same permissions to others, but each should have a separate login and password.

Assigning permissions in Miva Merchant is done by creating user accounts, establishing groups of privileges, and assigning users to those groups. A user can belong to one group or several groups, since each group can encompass different privileges.

Adding Users

Users are added to the Mall, not the store. Then they are assigned permissions for the actual store. Unless other users have been given the proper permission, only the store administrator may add new users.

STEP BY STEP

1. In the Admin Menu click the ▶ next to **Users**. This link will be above where you work on the store's settings.

2. Click the **Add User** link.

3. Enter the **User Name** of the person who will use this login (no spaces or special characters).

4. Enter the **Password** for the account, and then enter it again to **verify the password**.

5. Set any other privileges.

> If the person is an **Administrator**, he or she will have the same privileges you do, except for creating more users. However, you can assign that privilege as well.

 An administrator has access to make changes to the entire mall. This includes modules, domain settings and any additional stores. You should only assign the permissions needed for each user, so not all users should have full Administrative permissions.

6. Click the **Add** button.

Editing Users

To edit a user's login, password, or other assignments when added (administrator and create users assignments only), simply click on the User's name and make the changes as if you were adding a user.

Creating User Groups

User groups are assigned to a store. This means if you have more than one store you can assign users to one store or more.

Chances are if you are just starting out with Miva Merchant, you won't be making all of your assignments now. However, you can always come back and edit these settings.

Here, we'll create a group for users who can manually add, view, modify and delete products.

STEP BY STEP

1. In the Admin Menu, click the ▶ next to **Stores**.

2. Click the ▶ next to the store to which you will add this administrative group.

3. Click the ▶ next to **Groups**.

4. Click the **Add Group** link.

5. Enter the **Group Name**.

6. To make this group able to add, modify and delete products, simply check off the four options on the **Products** row (View, Add, Modify, Delete).

7. Click the **Add** button.

Elements of Administrative Groups

The administrative user group has several elements, which means you can assign some privileges to some users, and different ones to others. For example, if three people need to be able to process orders, but are not allowed to add products or view customers, you can restrict their access. You can allow user to view information, but not make changes.

Here's a breakdown of the possible admin permissions, and what they mean if more than View is selected:

Affiliate Money – the user(s) can view, add, modify and/or delete affiliate payout info

Affiliates - the user(s) can view, add, modify and/or delete affiliates

Attribute Templates – the user(s) can view, add, modify and/or delete attribute templates

Availability Groups – the user(s) can create, modify and/or delete customers, categories and products from the availability groups

Privileges: Name	View	Add	Modify	Delete
Affiliate Money	□	□	□	□
Affiliates	□	□	□	□
Attribute Templates	□	□	□	□
Availability Groups	□	□	□	□
Categories	□	□	□	□
Countries	□	□	□	□
Currency Configuration	□	□	□	□
Customers	☑	☑	☑	□
Data Export Modules (OpenUI™ Menu)	□	□	□	□
Data Import Modules (OpenUI™ Menu)	□	□	□	□
Delete Expired Shopping Baskets (OpenUI™ Menu)	□	□	□	□
Encryption	□	□	□	□
Inventory	□	□	□	□
Logging Configuration	□	□	□	□
Miva Mailer	□	□	□	□
Miva Marketplace Configuration	□	□	□	□
Miva Marketplace Products	□	□	□	□
Miva Marketplace Reports	□	□	□	□
OpenBatches™ Batch Management (OpenUI™ Menu)	□	□	□	□
OpenDesigner™ Management (OpenUI™ Menu)	□	□	□	□
OpenLanguages™ Management (OpenUI™ Menu)	□	□	□	□
OpenMaintenance™ Database Management (OpenUI™ Menu)	□	□	□	□
OpenOrders™ Order Management (OpenUI™ Menu)	□	□	□	□
OpenUI™ UI-Settings Backup (OpenUI™ Menu)	□	□	□	□
OpenUI™ UI-Settings Restore (OpenUI™ Menu)	□	□	□	□
OpenUI™ Update Wizard	□	□	□	□
Order Fulfillment Configuration	□	□	□	□
Order Processing	☑	□	□	□
Payment Configuration	□	□	□	□
Price Groups	□	□	□	□
Products	☑	□	☑	□
Sales Tax	□	□	□	□
Shipping Configuration	□	□	□	□
States	□	□	□	□
Store Settings	□	□	□	□
Store Utility Configuration	□	□	□	□
Store Utility Modules (OpenUI™ Menu)	□	□	□	□
System Extension Configuration	□	□	□	□
Upsold Products	□	□	□	□
User-Defined Links (OpenUI™ Menu)	□	□	□	□

This administrative group can work with customers, edit products and view orders.

Categories – the user(s) can add, modify and/or delete categories (this will not delete the products within those categories

Countries - the user(s) can add, modify and/or delete countries that are listed for customers to select

Currency Configuration – the user(s) can add, modify and/or delete any currency methods acceptable at the store

Customer – the user(s) can add, modify and/or delete any customers; user(s) can add customers manually, whether or not the person has shopped the store

Inventory – the user(s) can add, modify and/or delete settings for inventory tracking, default stock levels and messages

Logging Configuration – the user(s) can add, modify and/or delete any of the two logging configurations you may have set with your store

Order Fulfillment Configuration – the user(s) can add, modify and/or delete customer notification or merchant notification of orders (via e-mail), or any third-party fulfillment modules which may have been installed

Order Processing – the user(s) can add, modify and/or delete orders and batches

Payment Configuration – the user(s) can add, modify and/or delete the payment method modules, such as credit card methods or check options

Price Groups – the user(s) can add, modify and/or delete products or customers from specific price groups

Products – the user(s) can add, modify and/or delete products from the store

Sales Tax – the user(s) can add, modify and/or delete the assignments for adding sales tax to orders

Shipping Configuration – the user(s) can add, modify and/or delete any of the shipping methods

States – the user(s) can add, modify and/or delete any states from the list the shopper selects from when entering his or her billing or shipping address

Store Settings – the user(s) can add, modify and/or delete the store, as well as change colors, fonts, pagination, messages and other functions found in the settings when you click on the link to the store in the admin menu

Store Utility Configuration – unless given admin privileges, a user assigned to this section will not be able to import or export data, pack data files or delete expired shopping baskets

System Extension Configuration – the user(s) can add, modify and/or delete any system extension modules, including third-party modules, which may have been installed

Upsold Products – the user(s) can add, modify and/or delete any upsale items from the store

Editing Groups – Assigning Users

After adding a Group, you will need to assign any users you previously created in order for the proper permissions to be applied. If you do not assign a user to a group, and do not give the user full admin permissions, the user will be able to login to the Miva Merchant Admin Area, but will not be able to perform any tasks.

STEP BY STEP

1. In the Admin Menu, under your store, click the ▶ next to **Groups**.

2. Click the **Group** link you want to edit.

3. Click the **Users** link.

4. Use the checkboxes to assign or remove **Users**.

If you have a long list of users you can click the **Assigned** button to view users assigned to the group and the **Unassigned** button to see any users who are not assigned.

5. Click the **Update** button.

✔ *If you are editing an existing group and want to change the permissions, just click on the Group link. You can change the permissions of the group at any time.*

Deleting Groups

To delete a group of assigned permissions, simply click the ▶ next to **Groups**, click on the group's name, and click the **Delete** button.

No users will be deleted from the actual mall in this process.

Importing Products from a Flat File

If you have more than 20 products to sell, chances are you've found the process of adding products one by one to be nothing short of time consuming. That's why there is an import function to upload several products at once.

It is not necessary to create your categories in the Admin Area first, but it does make the process of importing products more productive. If you do not create categories first you will need to assign the imported products to the categories one at a time later via the Admin, or re-import products with their category assignments.

✔ **If you are a new computer user, the following procedures may be difficult. This means of importing products is not necessary, but saves time as it eliminates the need to add products through the product screens one at a time.**

Creating a Products File

After creating any needed categories in Admin, you need to create the products file, or database. This will include all the information shoppers will see when they visit the store: Name, Price, Description, Images, etc.

We'll use Microsoft Excel as an example because most people have a spreadsheet program, and Microsoft Excel is the most popular. If you plan to create your file in Microsoft Access, or another database program, you can follow the same structure—if you understand databases, then this should be relatively easy.

If you are using a spreadsheet program, you want to make sure you only have one worksheet for the file. Otherwise, you might get an error when attempting to save the file as text only.

The file we will ultimately import will not contain column headings, so if you do use them now, you will need to delete that row before importing. If you import the headings row, you'll find that Miva Merchant will import it as a product.

Your spreadsheet should look something like this:

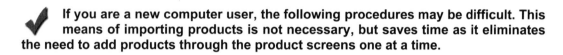

	A	B	C	D	E
1	1001	COUNTRY_NEW	Garth Brooks: DoubleLive CD	This CD is a f	24.99 graph
2	1002	COUNTRY_NEW	Garth Brooks: Chase CD	One of the be	14.99 graph
3	1003	COUNTRY_CLAS	Johny Cash: Greatest Hits	Take the wee	27.99 graph
4	1004	APPAREL	NJ Rockin' Tee	This all-cottor	16.00 graph

Aside from the **Product Code, Product Name** and **Price**, all other fields are optional. You may also include some fields for some products but not others. For example, if some products contain no images, you can leave the image field blank for those products.

Here, we show you all the available columns. We've labeled them A-Z as Microsoft Excel does.

A. **Product Code** – the item number; can contain letters, numbers, dashes and underscores (<u>cannot</u> contain spaces or any special characters)

B. **Category Code** – *not the name*, but the <u>code</u> used when creating the category

C. **Product Name** – try to keep the name brief

D. **Description** – try to refrain from using "quotes" if using Excel, as they can multiply themselves during export to a text file. However, you can always use a text editor to strip any quotation marks before importing to the store

E. **Price** – <u>do not</u> use a dollar sign ($) [this field must be formatted as a general number field with 2 decimals]

F. **Product Image** – unless you've changed the location, this will be entered like graphics/00000001/1001.jpg

G. **Product Thumbnail Image** – unless you've changed the location, this will be entered like graphics/00000001/1001a.jpg

H. **Taxable** – use a Yes or No if the item is taxable

I. **Weight** – if you are shipping according to weight, enter the weight of the product

J. **Cost** – if you are including the cost of the item (not price, but cost, such as wholesale cost) for account customers, then enter it here. This is not required.

K. **Available** - use a Yes or No if the item is to be viewed by the customer

L. **Attribute Template Code** – enter the code for an attribute template you may have created and want to assign to this particular product.

M. **Adjust Stock By** – for inventory, enter the negative or positive number of inventory to add or remove from the product's current count.

N. **Track Product Inventory** – Yes or No.

O. **In-Stock Message (Short)** – the short in-stock message for the product.

P. **In-Stock Message (Long)** – the long in-stock message for the product.

Q. **Track Low Stock Level** – Yes or No.

R. **Low Stock Level** – a positive number indicating the product's "low stock" status.

S. **Low Stock Message (Short)** – the short message indicating the product's inventory is low.

T. **Low Stock Message (Long)** – the long message indicating the product's inventory is low.

U. **Track Out Of Stock Level** – Yes or No

V. **Out Of Stock Level** – the positive number that indicates product is out of stock (usually 0 or 1)

W. **Hide Out Of Stock Products** – Yes or No to hide the product from the customer if out of stock.

X. **Out Of Stock Message (Short)** – the short message indicating the product is out of stock.

Y. **Out Of Stock Message (Long)** – the long message indicating the product is out of stock.

Z. **Limited Stock Message** – the text you want displayed if a customer orders more of one item than what you have on hand.

Saving the File

After entering all the pertinent information, you need to save the file as a delimited file. Unless you know how to work with advanced file types, we recommend saving it as a tab-delimited file. Be careful about saving your file using a simple comma delimiter—if you've used commas in your product descriptions, this could cause a huge mess during the import process.

In Microsoft Excel, and most other spreadsheet programs, you need to click on File... Save As... and select Tab-Delimited as the file type.

If you are using a database program, you may have to use an export feature to create a tab-delimited file. Refer to that programs help documentation for information.

After saving, you should now have two files – the original file (.xls if Excel), and the new file (.txt).

 If your new text file contains many "quotes" you may consider opening it in a text editor, such as NoteTab or NotePad. You can then do a Find & Replace, finding all "" and replacing with nothing (leave the replace box blank).

Importing the File

To import a flat file of products, you need to login to the Admin Area.

STEP BY STEP
---

1. In the Admin menu, click the ▶ next to **Stores**.

2. Click the ▶ next to the store to which you will be importing the file.

3. Click the ▶ next to the store's **Utilities** link (the first occurrence).

4. Click the ▶ next to **Import Data**.

5. Click the Import **Products From Flat File** link.

6. To locate the file on your computer, click the 📤 button. This will launch a new window that will let you upload the file from your computer.

7. Click the **Browse** button to launch another window showing your computer's directories.

8. Navigate to the directory where the text file is stored.

9. Click the name of the file you created, and then click the **Open** button. You will be returned to the Upload File window.

10. If the file has been imported before, check off the **Overwrite** box. Otherwise, you will not be able to import new products from this file.

11. Click the **Upload** button.

12. Click the **Next** button to move to the import screen.

Import Products From Flat File			
Existing Products:	⦿ Keep Existing Products ○ Update Existing Products ○ Replace Existing Products		
Attribute Templates:	⦿ Use ○ Copy		
Fields:	**Row** Product Code ▾	<Skip> ▾	<Skip> ▾
	1 MANZOOR1-2SMALLSPIKE	0	Y
	2 MANZOOR1SPIKE	0	Y
	3 0044-50380-2	0	Y
	4 0044-50413-9	1	Y
	5 006-2	1	Y

13. Choose what you would like to do with the existing products. You can:

   Keep Existing Products—any products already in your store will not be updated or affected in any way

Update Existing Products—if any products in this file you are importing carry different information than those already in the store, those products will be updated and will reflect the changes

Replace Existing Products—if any products in the flat file are already in the store, each product's data will be replaced with the information in the file. Any products in the store that are not in the flat file will remain in the store, unedited.

14. Choose if you would like to **Use** or **Copy** attribute templates. This will only apply if you are importing attribute template assignments. If you want the attributes for products automatically updated when you change the template, click the Use button.

15. Use the pull-down menus on each field to tell Miva Merchant what field it corresponds to in the store.

16. Click the **Import** button.

Depending on the number of items you are importing, along with your connection to the Internet, the import process could take from 10-15 seconds to a minute. If you receive timeout errors, and continue to do so, you can increase your ISP's timeout settings (contact your IHP/ISP) or you can break your largest file into smaller files for import.

Exporting Customers

You may want to export customers so you can devise a mailing list or import customer email addresses into a third-party bulk email program. Miva Merchant includes an option for exporting all customers who have created an account. The export file will not include any customers who may have placed orders without creating an account.

1. In the Admin Menu, click the ▶ next to your store name's link.

2. Click the ▶ next to the store's **Utilities** link.

3. Click the ▶ next to **Export Data**.

4. Click the **Export Customers to Flat File** link.

Export Customers To Flat File		
Export Customer to File: customers.dat		
Export:		
☑ Login	☑ Pass. Recovery Email	☑ Ship. First Name
☑ Ship. Last Name	☐ Ship. Email	☐ Ship. Phone
☐ Ship. Fax	☐ Ship. Company	☐ Ship. Address
☐ Ship. City	☐ Ship. State	☐ Ship. Zip
☐ Ship. Country	☐ Bill. First Name	☐ Bill. Last Name
☐ Bill. Phone	☐ Bill. Fax	☐ Bill. Email
☐ Bill. Company	☐ Bill. Address	☐ Bill. City
☐ Bill. State	☐ Bill. Zip	☐ Bill. Country
Delimiter: ⦿ Tab ◯ Other:		
If File Exists: ⦿ Append To File ◯ Replace File		
		Export Reset

5. Enter the name you would like the exported file to have.

6. Check off all the fields you'd like to include in the file. For example, if you will be importing the customer into an email program, we suggest exporting the billing name and email address. Keep in mind that each customer account record will include also shipping contact information, which may not be the person who actually placed an order. For this reason, you should consider only working with the billing information when using the file for marketing purposes.

7. Tell Miva Merchant if you would like to use the Tab delimiter or another delimiter.

    By default, the customers.dat file (the default file name for exported orders) is tab-delimited. This means the text file will contain a TAB SPACE between each field in the orders records. Tab-delimited files can usually be opened by any common spreadsheet or database program. However, if you know what you are doing, you can tell Miva Merchant to use a different delimiter, such as a comma or the pipe character.

8. Choose whether you'd like to append the customer list to any existing file you may have previously created, or to replace the file (if you are giving it the same file name).

    By default, exported data will append to the existing customers.dat file. This means any customers you export next week will automatically be added to the existing file, which includes all customers exported today. If you choose Replace File, then any previous exports to this specific file will be overwritten.

9. Click the **Export** button.

Retrieving Exported Customer

After exporting your customers, you'll want to get the **customers.dat** (or other file, if you changed the name) off the server and onto your computer.

The customers.dat file is located in the data directory on the server, and you will need to FTP or similar access to the server to get this file. For some, this file is located in the **mivadata** or **htsdata** folder off the web-accessed root of the server. This folder is supposed to be located outside the Merchant folder on root of your server (if it's not, contact your ISP).

Inside that data directory, you will need to navigate to the Merchant/0000000x/export directory. There you'll find the file (customers.dat or other file name).

Once you've found the file, you can download it to your computer (in ASCII mode), then import it into a spreadsheet or database program.

✔ **Whether or not the file is in the mivadata (or htsdata) directory, if you cannot access one of these folders on your server, you should contact your ISP – some restrict you from accessing folders on the root of the absolute server. This means no one, not even a developer, could help repair any database files that might be damaged if you make a serious mistake.**

Chapter Ten

Fleshing Out the Store

So far, everything you have learned will make your store operational. Chances are, however, you want to do a little (or a lot) more to make your online store unique and competitive. There are additional features in Miva Merchant that allow you to provide additional information and customized content to the customer. These are listed in no particular order, as each person will want different features and will want to make different changes.

Replacing Navigation Buttons

Miva Merchant's stock buttons aren't for every one. In fact, they've been used by so many stores operating completely "out of the box" that they are spotted a mile away.

You can change the buttons used for the **Navigation Bar** (the row of buttons at the top of each page of the store) with your own graphics.

| Store Front | Account | Search | Product List | Basket Contents | Checkout |

If you plan to create your own navigational buttons, they should be no taller than 25 pixels and no wider than 110 pixels to follow a standard design. *See Appendix B for sizing and graphics creation information.*

STEP BY STEP

1. In the Admin Menu, click on your store name's link.

2. Click on the **Images** link.

Body Background:	
Navigation Bar Logo:	graphics/en-US/mmui/blades.gif
Navigation Bar Logo Link:	http://www.mvcommerce.net
Navigation Bar "Select Store":	graphics/en-US/mmui/selstr.gif
Navigation Bar "Store Front":	graphics/en-US/mmui/storfrnt.gif
Navigation Bar "Account":	graphics/en-US/mmui/account.gif
Navigation Bar "Search":	graphics/en-US/mmui/search.gif
Navigation Bar "Product List":	graphics/en-US/mmui/prodlist.gif
Navigation Bar "Basket Contents":	graphics/en-US/mmui/basket.gif
Navigation Bar "Checkout":	graphics/en-US/mmui/checkout.gif

3. Next to the location of each button you would like to change, click the ⬟ button.

4. Click the **Browse** button.

5. Navigate to the directory on your computer that contains the new button.

6. Click on the new button's file, then click **Open**.

7. Click the **Upload** button.

Miva Merchant does have three other standard designs. They are called Olive, Hot Dog and Steel. These are also considered "out of the box" designs and don't really make your site unique from many others.

You can reach these other designs through the Wizards section for your store:

1. In the Admin Menu click the ▶ next to your store name's link.

2. Click the ▶ next to **Wizards** (the one beneath your store).

3. Click the **Look & Feel Configuration** Wizard link.

4. Follow the on-screen instructions.

Replacing Shopping Buttons

Throughout the store shoppers are faced with buttons (gray box with standard text) on which to click. The buttons are standard form buttons and perform the following functions:

♦ Add To Basket	♦ Previous
♦ Buy One Now	♦ Remove
♦ Continue	♦ Save
♦ Login	♦ Search
♦ Next	♦ Update

Miva Merchant allows you to choose how each button or action link is displayed. You can choose to display each as a **standard form button** (the gray box with text), an **image** that you have created, or to replace the text that is displayed on the form button.

If you want a truly custom look and feel for your online store, you probably want to create individual graphics for each of these buttons. When creating the graphics try to keep them uniform in design.

> ✔ *The Add to Basket button simply adds a product to the basket. The Buy One Now button adds a product to the basket and takes the shopper immediately to checkout. Most Miva Merchant users turn off the display of the Buy One Now button, so you may opt to not create a custom graphic for this button.*

STEP BY STEP

1. In the Admin Menu, click your store's link.

2. Click the **Buttons** link.

3. Make your selections for each button or link. If you want to use an image, you will need to click the ⬆ button and browse for the file and upload it to the store.

4. Click the **Update** button.

Modifying Display Features

You can make various changes in regard to what will be displayed on certain store screens. As with most other features, you can always edit the settings later.

Eliminating Miva Merchant's Navigation

You can choose to not display the navigation bar and/or the category tree. You might do this if you plan to create your own custom header for the entire store, which will include custom layout of custom graphical buttons.

STEP BY STEP

---

1. In the Admin Menu, click your store name's link.

2. Click the **Page Sections** link at the top.

3. Uncheck (or check) to turn on or off the navigation bar and category tree.

4. Click the **Update** button.

```
☑ Show Navigation Bar
☑ Show Category Tree
```

Customizing the Category Screen

You can customize how products are displayed on the Category Screen. Basic formats can be different for each category.

Miva Merchant's layout options for category screens is limited, but there are many third-party modules available to let you customize the display to your liking.

STEP BY STEP

---

1. In the Admin Menu, click the ▶ next to your store name's link.

2. Click the ▶ next to **Categories**.

3. Click the link for the category for which you want to change the product layout.

4. In the right-hand side, click the **Product Layout** link at the top.

```
Edit Category: Country Music                    ⊖ ⊛

Category  Pagination  Headers & Footers  Images  Product Layout
Products

Format:              Expanded ▾
Product Fields:      ☑ Product Name ☑ Product Code
                     ☑ Price          ☐ Weight
                     ☐ Description
Buttons:             ☑ Add One To Basket
                     ☑ Buy One Now
Image:               Thumbnail ▾
Inventory Level Message: Long ▾
```

5. Make selections according to what you want displayed, and whether or not you want products displayed as a list or in an expanded format.

> **Format** - choose Expanded (default display) or Line Item (list format with alternate shading)
>
> **Product Fields** - you can opt to turn on or off the Product Name, Code, Price, Weight and Description
>
> **Buttons** - you can opt to show or not show the Add One To Basket and Buy One Now buttons
>
> ✔ *The Buy One Now button adds a product to the basket and takes the shopper immediately to checkout. Most Miva Merchant users turn off the display of the Buy One Now button.*
>
> **Image** - you can opt to show the Thumbnail image, the Full Sized image, or no image at all
>
> **Inventory Level Message** – you can choose to display the Long or Short messages in reference to the inventory level messages you set for your store.

6. Click the **Update** button.

Customizing the Product List Layout

The product list is the list of items displayed when a shopper clicks on the Product List button. You can display the product list in the same way as category screens.

Stores with more than 100 products may not want to use this feature at all, as it's cumbersome to scroll through all the listings.

STEP BY STEP

1. In the Admin Menu, click your store name's link.

2. Click the **Product List Layout** link at the top.

3. Make any changes applicable.

> **Format** - choose Expanded (default display) or Line Item (list format with alternate shading)
>
> **Product Fields** - you can opt to turn on or off Product Name, Code, Price, Weight and Description
>
> **Buttons** - you can opt to show or not show the Add One To Basket and Buy One Now buttons

Image - you can opt to show the Thumbnail image, the Full Sized image, or no image at all

Inventory Level Message – you can choose to display the Long or Short messages in reference to the inventory level messages you set for your store.

4. Click the **Update** button.

Customizing the Search Screen Layout

The search layout affects the search results page. You can display the product list in the same way as category screens and the product layout.

STEP BY STEP
---

1. In the Admin Menu, click your store name's link.

2. Click the **Search Layout** link at the top right.

3. Make any changes applicable.

Format - choose Expanded (default display) or Line Item (list format with alternate shading)

Product Fields - you can opt to turn on or off Product Name, Code, Price, Weight and Description

Buttons - you can opt to show or not show the Add One To Basket and Buy One Now buttons

Image - you can opt to show the Thumbnail image, the Full Sized image, or no image at all

Inventory Level Message – you can choose to display the Long or Short messages in reference to the inventory level messages you set for your store.

4. Click the **Update** button.

Headers and Footers

We already learned about category and product headers and footers, but some other sections of your store may require additional information. For example, the Customer Login feature is nice, but wouldn't it be better if you explained to your customers the benefits of setting up an account?

You can assign headers and footers to various sections of your store. You can include headers and footers for the customer login screen, order screen, and other screens. **If you are using the KoolCat Look and Feel, turn to the end of this tutorial for Header and Footer information.**

To create Headers and Footers, **click on your store name's link** in the Admin Menu, then click on the **Headers and Footers** link.

```
Category Tree Header:    <P><B>Browse the Store:</B></P>



Category Tree Footer:    <P><B>Customer Service:</B></P>
                         <a href="../cserve.html">Customer Service</a><br>
                         <a href="../shipping.html">Shipping Info</a><br>
```

Headers and footers can include HTML, which means you can signify fonts, font sizes, even font attributes (such as **bold** and *italics*), as well as include image references. It's up to you, of course, to understand the coding of HTML; we have included a reference of basic commands you might use in **Appendix B**.

> ✓ *You could also use CSS. This requires a module to call in the style sheet. CSS has been found to work with most aspects of Miva Merchant and with most third-party modules. However, is not 100% supported, as there is no option to completely override all the font and other calls from the actual Miva Script files.*

Keep in mind that Headers and Footers are just that – collections of information (text and/or graphics) which will appear above or below the actual "meat" of the page. Be sure you don't take up too much space in your headers. Otherwise, customers will need to scroll through all the information before actually viewing products, category listings and other key content.

We've provided a detailed list of the headers and footers you can create, where they will appear, and some ideas on what information to include.

HEADER/ FOOTER	WHERE IT APPEARS IN STORE	WHAT TO INCLUDE?
Global Header	Adds a header to the entire store.	Store logo, customized navigation.
Global Footer	Adds a footer to the entire store.	Text links for the entire site, copyright info, company name, address & phone.
Category Tree Header	At the top of the categories list on the left-hand side of the screen.	Words like, "Choose a Category:"
Category Tree Footer	Below the category listing on the left-hand side of the screen.	A link to offline ordering info or contact page.
Customer Login Header	At the top of the page where a customer will either log into the store or create an account.	Prompt to create account, and reasons why.
Customer Login Footer	At the bottom of the page where a customer will log into the store or create an account.	Note about privacy issues.
Edit Customer Account Header	At the top of the page where a customer can edit his or her account information.	Tell customers what they can edit, and to be sure SAVE box is checked.
Edit Customer Account Footer	At the bottom of the page where a customer can edit his or her account information.	Remind customer to check SAVE box
Create Customer Account Header	At the top of the Account Creation page.	Remind customer that their information is privately held.
Create Customer Account Footer	At the bottom of the Account Creation page.	Remind customer that their information is privately held.
Missing Required Attribute(s) Header	When a customer does not select an attribute, a separate page will alert him or her to do so.	Explain that the customer should select an attribute, or just continue.
Missing Required Attribute(s) Footer	When a customer does not select an attribute, a separate page will alert him or her to do so.	Miva will state whether or not the attribute is required. Put your add'l info in the header or footer.
Search Header	At the top of the search page.	Tell customer he or she can search by product name, code, or description or price.

Search Footer	At the bottom of a search page.	Tell customers they can search by name, code, description or price.
Product List Header	At the top of the page which displays the product listing.	Tell customer to click the product code link to view the product page.
Product List Header	At the bottom of the page which displays the product listing.	Tell customer to click the product code link to view the product page.
Basket Contents Header	At the top of the basket page, which tells the shopper what is ready to be purchased.	Tell customer how to remove, or update the quantity of an item.
Basket Contents Footer	At the bottom of the shopper's basket page, which tells him or her what is ready to be purchased.	Tell customer how to remove, or update the quantity of an item.
Order: Customer Login Header	This page will appear if a customer who has not signed in wants to proceed to checkout.	Give a brief explanation of what a customer account is.
Order: Customer Login Footer	This page will appear if a customer who has not signed in wants to proceed to checkout.	Give a brief explanation of what a customer account is.
Order: Create Customer Account Header	Page appears if a customer who has not signed in attempts to checkout, then decides to create an account.	Explain your site's privacy issues, and exactly what information is stored.
Order: Create Customer Account Footer	Page appears if a customer who has not signed in attempts to checkout, then decides to create an account.	Tell the customer that next time he or she can simply sign in.
Order: Customer Information Header	This page displays the customer's shipping and billing contact information.	Ask customer to make any changes if necessary.
Order: Customer Information Footer	This page displays customer's shipping & billing contact info.	Same, or reiterate privacy policy.
Order: Upsale Header	If you offer upsale products, this will prompt the shopper to take advantage of the special offer.	Tell the customer this is optional, not required.

Order: Upsale Footer	If you offer upsale products, this will prompt the shopper to take advantage of the special offer.	Tell the customer this is optional, not required.
Order: Upsale Missing Required Attribute(s) Header	If a customer selects an upsale item that contains attributes, this page will appear.	Tell the customer he or she can select an attribute.
Order: Upsale Missing Required Attribute(s) Footer	If a customer selects an upsale item that contains attributes, this page will appear.	Tell the customer he or she can select an attribute.
Order: Select Shipping/Payment Header	This page contains the customer's order information, as well as prompts for shipping and payment method.	Ask the customer to select shipping and payment method below.
Order: Select Shipping/Payment Footer	This page contains the customer's order information, as well as prompts for shipping and payment method.	Tell the customer that shipping and payment selection is required.
Order: Payment Information Header	This page prompts the customer to enter the credit card or check number.	Ask customer to include this info so order can be processed.
Order: Payment Information Footer	This page prompts the customer to enter the credit card or check number.	Explain the format for entering this info.
Invoice Header	This page includes the final invoice/receipt.	Don't duplicate the Order Completed Message.
Invoice Footer	This page includes the final invoice/receipt.	Ask customer to print and save order.

Putting a Search Box on Every Page

Putting a search box on every page of your store can help potential customers locate items more quickly. It saves a step (visitors won't have to click on the Search button) and prompts the visitors to look for something they may want.

The form code used for your Miva Merchant store's search box can be extracted right from your store's search screen. Viewing the source code of the store page will give you the core code, which you can adjust to suit your needs.

Here's an example of the code we used to display a search box throughout and entire Web site. We've also made the search button a call to a graphic.

```
<FORM METHOD="post" ACTION="http://www.YOURDOMAIN.com/Merchant/merchant.mvc?">
<INPUT TYPE="hidden" NAME="Store_Code" VALUE="ENTERSTORECODEHERE">
<INPUT TYPE="hidden" NAME="Screen" VALUE="SRCH">
<INPUT TYPE="text" NAME="Search" SIZE="10" VALUE="">
<INPUT TYPE = "image" ALT = "click to search" SRC = "graphics/00000001/search.gif" BORDER = "0">
</FORM>
```

To shorten the width of the input box, you can change the line that denotes the SIZE. Be sure to test the front end form in both Netscape and IE, because each of these browsers translates those widths differently, depending on the versions of the browser.

We can now copy and paste the form into any header or footer for the store. The top of the category tree usually works well.

Existing Web Site Integration

Navigating from existing Web site pages to the online store should be seamless. Each area should look and feel, and function similarly so potential customers don't get lost or confused. If you already have an existing Web site and you want to carry that design into Miva Merchant, the first steps can be taken right in the Admin Area – using headers and footers and other elements.

If you don't yet have a design, you'll get a more seamless result if you first incorporate a design into the store, then generate your HTML pages off the results. This is discussed in a bit.

What about just using HTML pages?
Some prefer to use Miva Merchant solely as a shopping cart, and want to display all product information on individual HTML pages. This sounds like a great idea, but there are a few pitfalls to integrating your site and store this way:

♦ Each and every HTML page will require special coding for the Add to Basket link. If you use product attributes, additional form coding is needed. Miva Merchant will also need customization or a module to return the customer back to the HTML page after the item is added.

♦ You will still need to enter or import your products, along with any attributes, into Miva Merchant, thus doubling up on work.

♦ Shoppers who find their way into the store's product and category screens will get confused if the design and all pertinent information is not there, so you'd want to incorporate the overall design and functionality into the store anyway.

♦ If you want to use special features that require third-party modules, many of those features will not be available for your HTML pages.

There are also myths about Miva Merchant that prompt some store owners to use HTML pages instead of Miva Merchant for all product pages. The first is Search Engine Optimization. While years ago few search engines spidered Miva Merchant store screens, that is no longer the case. Google and other popular search engines will produce results from Miva Merchant stores, and many third-party modules have been developed to increase positioning based on formatted URLs and keyword integration.

A second myth is that you can't layout products the way you want in Miva Merchant. Not only can you use HTML to customize product pages, but third-party developers have even created template modules so you can layout the product, category, search, basket and other screens any way you wish. Some work by giving you selective options, while more robust ones let you use HTML and tokens to create a completely custom layout.

With a little research, you'll find that just about any issue one has about what Miva Merchant cannot do design wise can be done with either the Miva Merchant Admin features, a customization or a module.

And if you still want those HTML pages for SEO sake, there are modules that will auto-generate them for you.

So what are you telling me?
We're telling you to let Miva Merchant do it's job. Let Miva Merchant generate your categories and products. You'll save yourself a great deal of work, while still getting the results you desire.

Obtaining Store Links for Other Pages

You may want to hype products and provide store navigation on your Web site's standard pages. These are usually HTML pages, but may also carry file extensions of .shtml, .php, .asp, etc.

Main store links include those to the Storefront, Search, Product List, Basket and Checkout screens.

You can either copy and paste links from the browser address bar, or have Miva Merchant generate the links for you.

STEP BY STEP
---

    1.   In the Admin Menu, click on your store name's link.

    2.   In the upper right-hand corner, click the button.

> **Store Links For Store: MvCommerce.Net**
>
> **Store Front:** http://www.mvcommerce.net/Merchant2/merchant.mvc?Screen=SFNT&Store_Code=MVCShop
> **Search:** http://www.mvcommerce.net/Merchant2/merchant.mvc?Screen=SRCH&Store_Code=MVCShop
> **Product List:** http://www.mvcommerce.net/Merchant2/merchant.mvc?Screen=PLST&Store_Code=MVCShop
> **Basket Contents:** http://www.mvcommerce.net/Merchant2/merchant.mvc?Screen=BASK&Store_Code=MVCShop
> **Order Form:** http://www.mvcommerce.net/Merchant2/merchant.mvc?Screen=OINF&Store_Code=MVCShop
> **Customer Login:** http://www.mvcommerce.net/Merchant2/merchant.mvc?Screen=LOGN&Store_Code=MVCShop
> **Customer Add Form:** http://www.mvcommerce.net/Merchant2/merchant.mvc?Screen=ACNT&Store_Code=MVCShop
> **Affiliate Login:** http://www.mvcommerce.net/Merchant2/merchant.mvc?Screen=AFCL&Store_Code=MVCShop
> **Affiliate Add Form:** http://www.mvcommerce.net/Merchant2/merchant.mvc?Screen=AFAE&Store_Code=MVCShop

    3.   Click the links to make sure you are using the ones you need.

    4.   Copy and paste the links to your HTML pages.

You can use the same method to obtain the links for products and categories. Just open any product or category for editing and click the button.

> **Never just copy secure links from the browser's address bar. Secure links (for account and checkout, etc.) include a Session_ID string which identifies the shopping session. The Session_ID is unique for each shopper. Using these addresses to link to the store will result in shopping problems.**

Making the Storefront Your Site's Home Page

If you want to make your Miva Merchant Storefront Screen the actual home page to the entire Web site, there's the right way to do it. This is especially useful if you first incorporated a design into Miva Merchant and want to carry that same design throughout any supporting HTML pages.

Some people simply route the domain entry page to be the online storefront, but this can cause a hitch when you're trying to move up in search engines. If you plan to use this method, you should consult an SEO expert for assistance on making sure the page is coded properly.

STEP BY STEP

---

1. View your store's Storefront Screen via a Web browser.

2. On your browser's menu, choose to view the source code of the page. (For Internet Explorer, click on View... Source)

3. Select **ALL** the text (code), copy it and paste it in either an HTML editor or a plain text editor (such as NoteTab or NotePad).

4. Do a search in the file for the term **Session_ID**.

   The Session_ID is the variable that identifies each unique shopping session. Thus, the reference to it MUST be removed (leaving it will cause problems with shoppers, including some customers seeing other customers' information). There will usually be at least two references to this.

   The URL you will edit will look something like this:

   **https://www.yourdomain.com/Merchant2/merchant.mv?Session_ID=3BA8B63C000B7
   DE4000053B200000000&Screen=LOGN&Order=0&Store_Code=xxx**

   You **must** remove the entire string of :
   Session_ID=3BA8B63C000B7DE4000053B200000000&

   You will be left with this:
   https://www.yourdomain.com/Merchant2/merchant.mv?Screen=LOGN&Order=0&Store_C
   ode=xxx

   ✔ **Since Miva Merchant uses IF statements to determine where to send a shopper when he or she clicks the login or checkout links (ie. IF the shopper is logged in, send them to their account screen; IF NOT, send them to the login screen), you may want to remove the links to login and checkout from the home page completely. You cannot parse the IF statements in HTML pages. To do this, just remove the entire reference link and graphic.**

5. Save the file as index.html and upload it to the server.

Adding Links, Etc.
Miva Merchant places a base URL call at the top of each page it generates. If you view the source code of a Miva Merchant page, you will see:
<BASE HREF="http://www.xx.com/Merchant/>

This means that any relative link or image path you set will be called in relation to the Merchant directory. For more information on this, see below.

Using Relative Image Paths

There are two types of paths you can use to call images into your Web pages and via the Miva Merchant Admin (such as when assigning images manually, or placing images in headers and footers).

Direct paths reference a direct location on the server. Direct paths usually are entered as **/images/xx.gif**—whereas the images are located in the images directory off the root of the server (domain), or, **http://www.xx.com/images/xx.gif** - whereas a full URL is used to reference the file.

Relative paths reference a file based on its location in relationship to the current directory.

In your Miva Merchant store, you want to use **relative paths** when calling in graphics. Miva Merchant uses **Domain Settings**, which indicate what base URLs to use when a customer is in either secure or non-secure mode. Usually, the potential customer starts the shopping experience in non-secure mode. When he or she proceeds to the account or checkout screens, Miva Merchant automatically goes into secure mode. Miva Merchant does this by using those base URLs (and you'll see in the source code of the page what the BASE HREF is).

The base URL will look something like this:
http://www.xx.com/Merchant/ for non-secure pages
https://www.xx.com/Merchant/ for secure pages

Because customers may be viewing your images in both secure and non-secure mode, you need to use a relative path so that Miva Merchant can display the images properly. Using direct paths will result in customers being alerted that there are non-secure items on the page.

Also, going hand in hand, for your store, you should be putting your graphics somewhere in the /Merchant/ directory or a sub-directory within the main directory. (Anything uploaded via the Admin will, by default, go into the /Merchant/graphics/0000000X/ directory).

So, here's how you should call in images when using them in custom menus, navigation bars and headers and footers:

<IMG SRC="graphics/headers/xx.gif">

Here, we created a subdirectory inside the /Merchant/graphics/ directory, and named it "headers."

This relative path would be the same as:
http://www.xx.com/Merchant/graphics/headers/xx.gif for non-secure mode, and
https://www.xx.com/Merchant2/graphics/headers/xx.gif for secure mode.

You can use this same method if you are manually calling product images in any headers or footers, or in the Storefront Welcome Message. The proper call would be:

<IMG SRC="graphics/00000001/xx.jpg">

Keep in mind that since the /Merchant/ directory is already part of the base URL, you start your path assignment from a file or directory within the /Merchant/ directory. Because it's relative, it will be called directly in both secure and non-secure modes.

Relative paths can be used in hyperlinks as well!

There are other reasons to use relative paths. What if you switch hosts and put your store at a temporary address for a week? What if you change your domain name? Relative paths will keep everything working.

Chapter Eleven

MMUI Alternatives

The Miva Merchant User Interface (MMUI) does impose limitations when it comes to installing third-party modules (plug-ins) and customizations. Unless you understand Miva Script, you have to either learn coding techniques or pay someone to implement customizations for you. Nearly every fulfillment and system extension module requires coding for it to work with the MMUI. For this reason, alternatives are provided by third-parties.

OpenUI - The "Other" User Interface

An alternative interface, called the **Open Look & Feel (OpenUI)**, was not created by Miva Corp., but instead by a group of independent developers. It has, however, over the past few years, become a standard and though specific data is not available, likely more than half of all actively running Miva Merchant stores are running the OpenUI.

The OpenUI has widely become an acceptable alternative method by various developers and seasoned Miva Merchant users, and many Miva Merchant modules on the market actually require the OpenUI in order to work.

In the back end of Miva Merchant, it makes the module development and maintenance of the various files Miva Merchant needs to operate a simpler task for those familiar with the interface. However, the OpenUI renders useless any modifications you may have had someone make to the mmui.mvc file—one of the files that is essential to store operation. If you're a beginner and you're working with a new, clean store, chances are this won't apply.

In a nutshell, the OpenUI makes it easier for the user to install modules and not worry about losing changes when upgrading to new versions of Miva Merchant. There are compromises, however. Some sites notice a change in speed of the store itself. This is normally attributed to the type of server you are using, the amount of traffic you receive and how many customizations you have had made.

About the OpenUI

The OpenUI is an alternate user interface that can be used with Miva Merchant versions 2.0 and higher. A user interface is what controls how the store functions and, as a result, how it looks and feels. Thus, the term "Look and Feel."

By default, Miva Merchant uses the Miva Merchant User Interface (MMUI), also called the Miva Merchant Look & Feel. The mmui.mvc is one large file that contains all of the core functionality coding in order for your store to operate as it does. Additional files, called modules, "plug in" to Miva Merchant, allowing other things to happen.

For example, the meremail.mvc module tells Miva Merchant to send an order confirmation email to the merchant. The stdacct.mvc module tells Miva Merchant to allow for the running and display of a batch report.

Third-party modules must also "plug in" to Miva Merchant. However, under the MMUI, this usually requires coding changes. For example, in order to install a coupon redemption module, not only must the module itself be installed, but coding must be done to the mmui.mvc file—something must tell Miva Merchant to use that module. For uncompiled Miva Merchant (versions 4.13 and lower) the mmui.mvc file can be edited with a text editor. For compiled Miva Merchant (versions 4.14 and higher) a Compiler's Kit must be purchased from Miva Corp.

The OpenUI instead uses one core UI file and several supporting files. It uses "hook points," which allows developers to create modules that "hook in" to Miva Merchant. Therefore, while an MMUI store will require coding for the coupon module to prompt the customer to enter the coupon code, the OpenUI version of the same module will just "hook in." The developer will have the coupon module tell the OpenUI where to display this information.

Since the OpenUI modules are using hook points, they can simply be installed to the store and used immediately requiring no additional coding to the core MMUI file. In fact, once the OpenUI is installed properly, the MMUI file itself is not even used.

Benefits of the OpenUI...

The most prominent advantage of using the OpenUI is the ability to install features with little experience and not lose them when you upgrade.

> *With each new release of Miva Merchant —whether it be a complete upgrade or an update to an existing version—the mmui.mvc file is overwritten. This means in order to keep any changes made to the store, someone will need to recode the new mmui.mvc.*

With the OpenUI, the changes will not be lost. This is because the OpenUI uses hook points to call features in. Now, the third-party module may have to be upgraded, but since there were no coding changes that had to be made to make the module work, there are none overwritten.

 Though no changes will need to be made to make the upgraded third-party modules function as described. If you upgrade Miva Merchant any previously <u>customized</u> third-party modules may require additional work in order to function the same as before.

Another advantage of the OpenUI is that several modules today will only work with this user interface. For many developers, requiring coding in the mmui.mvc opens doors for additional support, since many inexperienced users have difficulty making coding changes. Also, the OpenUI has additional features, and those features can work with some of the modules.

A third, and very embraced advantage is the support of **tokens** (versions 4.0 and higher). Tokens are snippets of logical code that call in specific data, such as a product name, the price, the category name, etc. Tokens opened a whole new world because now Miva Merchant can layout areas of their store using HTML and tokens, placing product information and other information exactly where they want. Many template-style modules have been created to give users total control over every single aspect of the Miva Merchant front end.

The Look Itself, Remains

The OpenUI does not make Miva Merchant itself look, feel or act any differently that a standard user will notice. There are some additional features, but overall, nothing you've learned in this book will be for nothing. You'll still add products, implement price groups, and perform other tasks the same way. You will, however, see little icons denoting that the standard feature has been enhanced by the OpenUI.

OpenUI Concerns...

While there are advantages, there are also potential disadvantages. Here are some of the issues some have faced with the OpenUI. Fortunately, they're all avoidable.

Speed...

Some shared servers on shared hosting environments have noticed a slow down after installing the OpenUI. This is due to several Miva Merchant sites being hooked into one Virtual Machine or Empresa engine (which is required in order for Miva Merchant to run on the server), and server's not being configured to handle such multiple requests.

Generally, all stores will see a very small decrease in speed. In most cases this decrease is not enough to even notice.

Also, stores that have scores of modules will notice more of a decrease than those running just a few. However, this is due to the fact that more items need to be processed before Miva Merchant can return the page to the visitor. Again, it is usually not a major concern, but can be one on some shared hosting environments depending on the amount of traffic and server configuration.

✔ *A decrease in speed due to scores of modules is even noticeable on an MMUI store. It's logical—the more "things" that have to be processed, the longer it's going to take.*

If you have a concern about this, you should contact your host or a potential host and ask for example sites that use the OpenUI.

Confliction

Since the OpenUI uses "hook points" for nearly each specific task that is otherwise outlined in the MMUI, two modules that use the same "hook points" may conflict with each other. This depends on the module and the module developer.

Over the past years, many updates have been made to the OpenUI to add more hook points. And, in most cases, confliction can be attributed to either the installation of two modules that essentially do the same thing, or poor coding from an inexperienced developer.

Server Misconfiguration

Some host servers are not configured properly, which can lead to issues when initially installing the OpenUI. However, the OpenUI Consortium, has worked around known issues by providing alternative installation methods.

Additional Features of the OpenUI

The OpenUI offers some additional features built-in. Some are worth using the OpenUI even if you don't plan to add any third-party modules. Here are just a few:

1. **No Cookie Shopping**—allowing potential customers with cookies turned off to shop the store

2. **Time Zone Offset**—the date and time displayed for orders is based on the server's time zone. Now, your local time zone can be displayed.

3. **Payment Attempts**—Bye-bye, credit card hackers. The OpenUI lets you set options for failed payment attempts, such as forcing the visitor to wait for a specific time period before he/she can try another card.

4. **Select One options**—will make the words "Select One" the first option on attribute, payment and shipping pull-down menus.

The OpenUI includes other new features, as well as enhancements to Miva Merchant's existing features.

The Open Statistics feature (and add-on to the OpenUI) provides more enhanced store statistics.

Who Uses the OpenUI?

Anyone running a Miva Merchant store can use the OpenUI. Contrary to some host comments, nothing prohibits a merchant from switching to this alternative look and feel.

Some Miva Merchant users have concerns because many hosts say they don't support the OpenUI. The thing is, most hosts don't support third-party modules period. Anything other than Miva Merchant "out of the box" is above and beyond what most hosts want to deal with. And who can blame them? Additional support for products they don't sell means additional costs they don't want to incur. Support for the OpenUI and any other third-party module should come from the actual developer and/or retailer of the module(s).

Thus, you can use the OpenUI because it will run on Miva Merchant period—there is no "edition" of Miva Merchant that rejects it, only servers that may not be configured properly so it can be installed (even then, the developer has produced special install files for specific hosts that are available upon request).

While there's no hard numbers released on just how many stores use the OpenUI compared to those that don't, we can say that the results of those who don't couldn't be attributed solely a lack of choosing the OpenUI— many newer users don't run it because they've yet to encounter its presence. Most stumble across it while looking for a module, finding out that it either requires the OpenUI, or that they can install the module without coding if they run the OpenUI.

Also, a high percentage of module sales through the top Miva Merchant developers and retail outlets are attributed to the OpenUI opposed to the MMUI. We're talking more than three-quarters of module buyers are purchasing for OpenUI usage. That's a big number.

So, who uses the OpenUI? Small Mom-N-Pop shops to large corporations rely on the user interface so they can run key third-party solution.

How to Get the OpenUI

The OpenUI can be purchased from an approved reseller. The cost as of August 2004 is just $40. Some developers and retailers offer installation (because it requires first backing up files and host configurations can get in the way) .

Installing the OpenUI

The process of installing the OpenUI itself is pretty simple, especially if no customizations (that includes adding headers or footers, setting fonts, etc.) have been made to your Miva Merchant store.

However, since the installation process requires a connection between your server and a third-party server providing the latest OpenUI files, connection problems may arise. That's why it is so important to backup essential data files before installing the OpenUI. Since installation requires that your host server is configured correctly and will not timeout before the files are transferred, as well as the traffic load on the other server providing the files, issues can and do arise. Failed installations are usually a result of a host server problem.

Installation instructions are included with the OpenUI files. However, many users have great concern about their store's data files, and opt to have a third-party developer install the look and feel for them.

Once the OpenUI is installed, however, most all other third-party modules will just plug…and play, requiring no more needs to pay someone else for additional module installations.

DynamicTemplates

Copernicus Business Systems offers up their own engine that functions with both the MMUI and the OpenUI. The DynamicTemplate Engine uses template files for all the screens in the Miva Merchant store, and supports most modules that use OpenUI tokens.

The engine was initially designed to be used in conjunction with the OpenUI, but the company has now expanded its use to work with MMUI stores. However, not all third-party modules will work with the engine. Most do, but you would need to contact developers to inquire first.

Back to its roots, however, many OpenUI stores run DynamicTemplates as well because it gives more control over the look and feel of the site as a whole, allowing modules to be called into exact locations so the displays on the screen are exactly as desired.

DynamicTemplates also allow the creation of new screens for the store. In fact, every single product, category and other page can run off its own individual template.

Who Uses DynamicTemplates?

The most common users of DynamicTemplates are Miva Merchant compiled (versions 4.14+) users who opt not to use the OpenUI, and OpenUI users who want even more control over every single aspect of their online store. Most who use DynamicTemplates spend a significant amount of time getting their templates just right because they want their store to be the absolute best it can be.

How Do I Get It?

DynamicTemplates can be purchased from an approved reseller. As of August of 2004, the cost is $99.95

Chapter Twelve

Store Add-Ons

Chances are when you purchase a new car there are some other goodies you want that aren't included. Okay, maybe you aren't looking to mount a hula girl on the dash, but a bracket for your cell phone, or a compass on the dash board may be in order. These are add-ons that aren't available "out of the box" but can easily be integrated.

There are hundreds of available add-ons for Miva Merchant, even some that run independently.

Miva Corporation itself has developed various tools to ease the process of payment solutions, marketing, bulk emailing and even synching data with QuickBooks. Some of them are already available through your Miva Merchant Admin Area, but cannot be utilized before signing up for the service.

Miva Marketplace

Realizing that online merchants need more than just an online store, Miva Corp. developed Miva Marketplace. The feature is an automated marketing service integrated with Miva Merchant that drives targeted shoppers to your store. Introduced in version 4.10, it lets you advertise products effectively, only paying for what is actually viewed by potential customers.

Miva Marketplace is driven by the FindWhat.com Network. It's a no risk pay-per-click system, which means you only pay for the highly targeted traffic that actually visits your store. And, since you set the price you are willing to pay for the traffic, as well as a maximum budget amount, you maintain complete control about how much is spent advertising your products.

Previously, Miva Marketplace could only serve actual product listings to targeted shoppers. Now, you can provide keyword placements, which means the program will work with HTML pages as well. In fact, you can setup and use Miva Marketplace before your store is even launched.

How It Works

Miva Marketplace is a pay-for-performance search engine. After signing up and bidding for results, merchants are sent traffic.

As a merchant, you bid for placement of your listings. For example, if the current bid for top results of the search "lawn mower" is 25 cents, you can bid 30 cents to be placed first. When potential customers search using this particular term, your listing will appear at the top of the list. You only pay for that particular listing if someone clicks on the link to your site.

Who Sees the Ads

Every day tens of millions of ads and listings are powered by the FindWhat.com Network, which means your listings are served through major shopping directories as well. Miva Marketplace ads are targeted to existing shoppers.

Joining Miva Marketplace

Miva Marketplace works with Miva Merchant versions 3.0 and higher. The host company of the site must have the commerce library for this featured installed.

STEP BY STEP

1. In the Admin Menu, click the **MAIN** link to return to the main Admin screen.

2. Scroll down to the Wizards area and click the **Miva Marketplace Signup Wizard**.

   ✔ *If you already have a FindWhat.com account, you need not create a separate signup. See below for enacting your account in Miva Merchant.*

3. Click the **Next** button.

4. If prompted, accept the default host URL, or enter any special URL you may have been provided.

5. Click the **Next** button.

6. If prompted, select **New Account**, then click the Next button.

7. Follow the steps to complete the application process, which include password creation and entering billing information.

For Existing FindWhat.com Users

You can use your existing account with Miva Marketplaces.

STEP BY STEP

1. In the Admin Menu, click the ▶ next to **Marketing**.

2. Click the **Miva Marketplace** link.

3. Enter your FindWhat.com Username and Password.

4. Click the **Update** button.

Adding Individual Products to Miva Marketplace

You can optionally include any products in your store in the Miva Marketplace directory. Since you can set individual options for each product, you don't have to add limited items that may not stay in stock. You can instead focus on key products.

STEP BY STEP
---

1. In the Admin Menu, click the **Products** link.

2. Find the product you want to add to Miva Marketplace and open the product for editing.

3. Click the **Miva Marketplace** link at the top of the product's edit screen.

4. Set the various options for the product.

   For the product to be listed with Miva Marketplace, you must check the **Create Miva Marketplace Listing For This Product** box.

   Keyword Ad Title—by default, this is the product name. You can make changes here.

   Description—You can create an optional description of the product. This should be text only.

   If the item is of an adult nature, you must check off the **Adult Content** box.

   Maximum Price/Click—enter the amount you are willing to pay for each click as a result of this item being listed. Do not include the currency symbol.

   Keywords—enter any keywords for the product, with each separated by a comma.

5. Click the **Update** button.

After updating, the Miva Marketplace listing will go into a pending status.

Managing Your Miva Marketplace Account

After creating your account, you can manage product listings, view reports, manage keywords and more.

All the options can by accessed by clicking the ▶ next to Marketing in the Admin Menu, then by clicking the ▶ next to Miva Marketplace.

Miva Mailer

This feature was introduced in version 4.13, and lets you send targeted emails to customers, affiliates and more. It's a great feature for merchants using hosts that won't allow for bulk emailing of customers. Since the email is actually sent from the Miva Network, it also means no bandwidth charges are incurred by you.

Miva Mailer does carry a fee, ranging from about $7.50 to $50.00 per month, all dependent on how many email messages you plan to send.

How It Works

Miva Mailer sets an opt-in box for customers (or affiliates), which is displayed when they create an account, update their account, or checkout from the store. Only customers who opt-in can receive email you plan to send. If they do not opt-in, they will receive nothing through Miva Mailer.

The store administrator can then create either text or HTML-formatted emails to send to the list of subscribers. These emails can be personalized with the customer or affiliate name, and most other information.

Once the email is created, you can schedule the send time, which means you can create the email on a Monday, and schedule it to be sent on Wednesday.

Signing Up for Miva Mailer

To signup for Miva Mailer:

1. Click the **MAIN** link in the Admin Menu.

2. Click the **Miva Mailer Setup Wizard** in the main Admin Area.

3. Follow the instructions for signup.

After signing up, you can access the features, as well as assistance on Miva Mailer, by clicking the ▶ next to **Marketing** in the Admin Menu, then by clicking the ▶ next to **Miva Mailer**.

Miva Synchro

Users of QuickBooks can benefit from this new feature, which synchs products, inventory and customers, and orders. Miva Synchro will synch with QuickBooks Premiere or Pro and Miva Merchant.

How It Works

Miva Synchro, when installed on your computer, communicates with Miva Merchant through an Internet connection and a module (installed in the Miva Merchant Admin). When initiated (at scheduled intervals or manually) it can download your store's orders into QuickBooks, as well as update any customer information. It can also synch product information between the two applications.

The program includes field mapping capability, so you can map fields in QuickBooks to fields in Miva Merchant, and vice versa.

Miva Synchro can even synch inventory, which means if you take phone and mail orders through QuickBooks, then the inventory can be synched right with Miva Merchant, providing a more realistic inventory count online.

The process can also be integrated with Miva Mailer to notify existing customers (in QuickBooks) of account logins for the online store.

How To Signup

Miva Synchro must be purchased from Miva Corp. Pricing as of August 2004 is $399.

Third-Party Solutions

Since Miva Corporation opened the doors for other companies and individuals to develop modules (plug-ins) for Miva Merchant, hundreds of other features are available, with many more being developed regularly.

It's great news for Miva Merchant users, and it is a key reason many online merchants switch to Miva Merchant. Most other e-commerce software developers restrict outside development, and many who allow third-parties to get a piece of the pie do so only by first charging hefty start-up costs.

Over the years, Miva Corp. has come to even embrace many third-party developers, meaning you, the end-user, get a vast selection of add-ons to choose from. There are some companies that focus solely on Miva Merchant.

When considering third-party solutions, you should first turn to a list of Miva Corp.'s Certified Business Partners. You'll find a directory online at: **www.miva.com/partners**

What is a Module?

In laymen's terms, a module is a piece of software that plugs into Miva Merchant and provides additional features. Any module you consider purchasing and/or installing should be from a Miva Partner, because partners are required to follow specific guidelines.

Types of Modules

There are various types of modules, and since you've already learned how the core of Miva Merchant works, you'll understand these.

Fulfillment Modules
These types of modules assist in order fulfillment and include features like coupon or gift certificate redemption, special email notifications, and order status modules. They are, after being installed to the mall, usually assigned to the store under Order Fulfillment.

Discount Modules
These module types provide ways to offer special discounting, such as percentage savings when a certain subtotal amount is reached.

Shipping Modules
These types of modules provide various shipping configuration options, such as giving the ability to configure shipping based on the country or state in the Ship To address, or providing a real-time gateway with FedEx or the USPS.

Payment Modules
These modules configure additional payment options, such as money order, PayPal and split payment methods.

Store Functionality Modules
These modules provide additional functional enhancements. Some examples are a basket display on all store pages, navigation enhancements and other features that provide visitors with the ability to shop more easily.

Admin Utilities Modules
From custom batch reports or import and export modules, these utility modules help you on the Back-End.

Look and Feel Modules
These modules provide various options, giving you the ability to create a custom look and feel (design) for your store. Some handle the entire overall shell of the store, while some add little, yet noticeable, features.

What to Expect from Third-Party Developers

You, as a customer of a third-party developer, should have certain expectations, the most important being that the developer has followed the guidelines of development set forth by Miva Corp. That's why it's important to purchase from Certified Business Partners.

Any Third-Party Module you purchase should include instructions on how to use it, including which menus to use, and how to set the options. If you purchase a module that does not include such instructions, you should contact the developer or company you purchased it from immediately.

Once you have researched and decided on a module, there are some things to consider.

▶ An expectation of some third-party modules is the requirement to edit the .mvc files which keep Miva Merchant intact. This can become tedious (and sometimes dangerous) for those who do not understand Miva Script.

If you plan to purchase third-party modules that require modifications of any of the essential .mvc files, you should consider paying for the developer to install the module, or hire a different coder or developer to install it for you. Ideally, you shouldn't be touching these files at this point.

Or, you can consider first installing the **Open Look and Feel** (OpenUI), which will make most all modules just plug in and run, eliminating the need for coding. The OpenUI is discussed in the next section.

▶ The ideal module will install itself, and will use the admin interface to allow you to customize the features. Unfortunately, since Miva Script is so complex, this type of development usually throws many hurdles in the developer's way. Just because some modules require additional work does not mean they are less superior. Some modules require some editing, but are less expensive than others with a more elaborate interface.

Adding Third-Party Modules

The only installation we discuss in this book is that of a module that works directly with Miva Merchant and will require no coding. However, it's always wise to first read the documentation of a module for any special instructions.

STEP BY STEP
---

1. In the Admin Menu, click the ▶ next to **Modules** at the top of the menu.

2. Click the **Add Module** link.

3. Click the ⬦ button to navigate your computer and find the module OR, enter the path to the module (i.e. modules/ui/xxx.mvc), according to the directions that came with the module.

4. Click the **Add** button.

After adding a module to the domain (or, mall) it will need to be assigned to the store. Many new users skip this step and wonder why a module is not doing anything for their store. Follow the instructions provided by the developer to see where to activate the module for the store.

Chapter Thirteen

Working Offline

Once your Miva Merchant store is live, you don't want to use it as a testing ground. Slow Internet connections can also get in the way of performing tasks.

Many of the things you develop for your store will provide better results if first worked with offline.

Create Items, then Import

Miva Merchant includes a product import module. Third-party developers have created import modules for many other tasks, such as importing categories and customers, and exporting existing products so you can edit them and re-import once changes are made.

Besides speeding up the process, working with data offline lets you work in private. When you add products manually via the Miva Merchant admin, customers can ultimately see the items before you've made any additional edits, such as creating attributes or setting inventory counts.

To import items you'll need to create a flat file, which can derive from a spreadsheet or database program.

Test HTML First

If you plan to use HTML in your headers, footers or for product descriptions, it is wise to use an offline editor (either an HTML or plain text editor) and test the content in a browser before putting it online. This will help eliminate potential customers from seeing errors, which do often occur.

The best practice is to view the source code for your Miva Merchant storefront, and copy the <HTML>, <HEAD> and <BODY> sections into a dummy template file, then work with that. Then, you can reference graphics and links relatively and test them outside your store (using an Internet connection, as the relative links would actually be pointing to your store). When placing content in the store, only copy the content between the <BODY> tags. Miva Merchant will dynamically create the page.

Use Miva Mia

Whether you have a slow Internet connection, or just want to make product and other updates before making them live in the store, you may decide to work with Miva Merchant offline. **Miva Mia** is an engine that allows both users and developers to work offline. You can add products, change headers and footers, even manipulate your design, then upload everything to the server when complete.

Miva Mia is considered to be an advanced method of working offline with Miva Merchant. To use it, you must know how to FTP and you must keep track of the files you need to both download and upload.

What is Miva Mia?

Miva Mia is software installed on your local computer, turning your computer into a low-volume "web" server, running the engine that allows Miva Script files to be parsed by the browser. It is available for free from Miva Corp.'s Web site.

Why Would I Use It?

There are many reasons you may choose to install Miva Mia on your computer.

1. **Speed**—When you make changes to your Miva Merchant store, you are doing so via an Internet connection, which means you have to wait for screens to load and reload when updating. If you are using a dial-up connection, this can be cumbersome.

2. **To Test Before Publishing**—You may want to view your product and category pages, as well as other screens, before they are live to the Internet. Miva Mia lets you work offline, test away, then upload everything once you're happy with the results.

3. **To Demo Modules**—Some third-party developers offer demos of modules that will only work with Miva Mia.

4. **To Pack Data**—Some stores with data files that are large in size may get timeouts when trying to pack the data. Packing offline eliminates Internet connections and server timeouts that may be getting in the way.

Many developers and designers use Miva Mia to test modules, scripts and client sites before they go live.

With Miva Mia, the core features of Miva Merchant will work the same as they do when run live off a Web server. Some features, such as email and third-party modules may not work seamlessly running under Miva Mia.

Where Do I Get It?

Miva Mia is available from **www.miva.com** for free. You simply register, receive a license key and download the software.

There are also some third-party software programs available that allow you to create and edit store content offline, then update the store in one fell swoop. Consider your needs then evaluate your options.

Chapter Fourteen

Troubleshooting the Store

Just like anything else in life, setting up and building a Miva Merchant store is not foolproof. If you've followed each and every step in this book, and documented any specific settings needed, troubleshooting any issues should be fairly simple.

Here we will discuss some of the most common issues regarding basic Miva Merchant errors and mistakes. After each, we outline steps to take, in order, in hopes to resolve the issue.

Troubleshooting Email

ISSUE:
The merchant (you) does not receive an email when customers place orders.

- ◆ Check to make sure the **Merchant Notification** option is setup under **Order Fulfillment Configuration**.

- ◆ Check to make sure you are using the right **Mail Server** under **Domain Settings**. This is usually your hosting provider's sendmail server. Check with your IHP.

ISSUE:
The customer does not receive email confirmation of an order.

- ◆ Make sure the **Customer Notification** is setup under **Order Fulfillment Configuration**.

- ◆ Check to make sure you are using the right **Mail Server** under **Domain Settings**.

- ◆ Make sure the customer entered the right email address.

- ◆ Ask the customer if there have been any other email problems with his or her ISP, such as a full mailbox, or incorrect password.

- ◆ Make sure you are not on a list of sites accused of spamming.

ISSUE:
The customer or merchant email does not line up – the information all runs together.

 ♦ Make sure you are not entering HTML in the email configuration box.

 ♦ Some email clients auto-format emails their own way. There's not a lot you can do for the customers other than direct them to check their email settings.

ISSUE:
Why isn't the payment information in the merchant email?

 ♦ For secure transactions, the payment information can only be accessed by logging into admin. Email is not secure.

Troubleshooting Attributes

ISSUE:
The customer sees the list of attributes, but no prices assigned to them until checking out.

 ♦ When entering each attribute, type the additional amount (or total amount) in this field as well. The additional amount you signify in the additional cost field is not displayed on the product page.

ISSUE:
Even though the attribute is not required, the customer is taken to a second screen, telling the customer that all attributes in bold are required.

 ♦ By default, Miva Merchant will do this if an attempt is made to add an item to the basket from a screen that does not display the attributes to the customer. This is done in case a customer failed to realize there were additional options.

Troubleshooting Availability Groups

ISSUE:
Only the assigned customer sees the category of products. However, when anyone searches the store, the products appear in the search results list.

 ♦ Even if you assign a category, you must also assign the products to the availability group.

ISSUE:
The customer is logged in, but cannot see the items that have been assigned to the group.

♦ Make sure the customer is assigned to the group.

♦ Make sure the customer does not have two login accounts, one which might not be assigned to the group.

Troubleshooting Customer Accounts

ISSUE:
The customer has lost his or her password.

♦ Instruct the customer to request, from the login page, for the password to be emailed.

♦ Reset the password in the admin area for the customer.

ISSUE:
The customer wants to close his or her account.

♦ Delete the customer from the customer accounts area in the Admin area.

ISSUE:
Other shoppers are being treated as if they logged in, and are unknowingly pulling up others accounts while they shop.

♦ Make sure you have not used any links for static web pages which include the Session_ID in them.

♦ Make sure you follow the proper procedure if using Miva Merchant links on static web pages.

♦ Make sure there aren't two customers using the same computer to shop around and not check out.

♦ Try to pack the store's data to see if you have duplicate key corruption.

Troubleshooting Category Pages

ISSUE:
I'm using subcategories, and the main category pages are completely blank. What should I put there and how do I do it?

♦ The headers and footers feature in the Category section is perfect for this. You can hype products, or provide your own graphical links to those subcategories.

♦ Consider a third-party module that will automatically display all the subcategories in a list format in this area.

ISSUE:
The category pages take forever to load.

♦ How many products are displaying? If it's more than 10, try paginating the categories.

♦ How large in size (kilobytes) are your thumbnail images?

Troubleshooting Secure Connections

ISSUE:
When trying to check out the error "modules/ui/mmui.mv: Line 2802: MvDO: Runtime Error: Error opening 'lib/db.mv': No such file or directory" is received.

♦ The secure URL is not setup correctly. Check the domain settings for the mall.

♦ Check with your hosting provider to be sure you are using the right URL.

ISSUE:
Customers are receiving the message: "SECURITY ALERT: name on site certificate doesn't match name of site."

♦ You are not using a secure certificate registered to you. You will probably have to purchase a certificate from reputable firm, or check with your hosting provider to see if it offers certificates which signify you as the user.

ISSUE:
When a customer goes to checkout, they see a message that says not all items are secure.

♦ Make sure you've referenced all graphics relatively.

Appendix A
Installing Miva Merchant

There are two steps to setting up Miva Merchant itself on the server. First, the files that make Miva Merchant run, are uploaded or extracted in your host directory for your domain. Then, the Miva Merchant setup process is run, which actually installs Miva Merchant for use, including the creation of database files.

If you obtained your Miva Merchant license from as part of a hosting package, chances are Miva Merchant has already been installed on your server.

If the Miva Merchant files have been put in place but the setup script has not been run, you'll need to skip ahead to the **Miva Merchant Setup** section.

Installing Miva Merchant

Placing the Miva Merchant script and data directories on the server is actually a simple process, providing your hosting provider has given your domain the proper authorization to use the Miva Empresa server (also known as the Virtual Machine for compiled Miva Merchant), and **providing you are familiar with FTP and directories**. If you are not, you should hire someone to do this for you.

Miva Empresa is what allows Miva Script to work on a server. Without it, your shopping cart program is useless. If your host does not provide Miva Empresa or the Virtual Machine, you can work on installing it yourself or work with a developer. If you are not allowed to do this on your host account, you will need to find a Miva-enabled host.

Downloading the Right Files

Once you purchase a copy of Miva Merchant from either Miva Corp. or a reseller, you should receive a registration number and access to downloading a zipped (or tarred—extension .tar) or an executable file that contains all the necessary files.

Likely, you want to download the latest version. You'll find the latest release information at Miva's web site at www.miva.com.

If you are provided with a .exe file, you will extract this on your local computer, then upload the files to the server. If you are provided with a .tar file, you can upload this file directly to the server and extract it there—it will create all the directories and subdirectories for you. For .tar files, you need TELNET or Secure Shell access so you can run a line command.

Installing via .exe File

After downloaded the .exe file, you run it on your computer. Simply open the file and accept the defaults for installation, except at the last screen, it's best if you choose not to run the setup files (this is for using a local copy of Miva, and if you're a beginner, you won't be doing this yet).

The .exe will extract all the files to a directory on your computer (in Windows, this is usually C:\Program Files\Miva for PCs). All of the files in this folder need to be uploaded to your server.

STEP BY STEP

1. Connect to your server via FTP.

2. In the **HTML** directory (where your index.html file is located), create a new folder and name it Merchant (or anything else you'd like to call it – by default most hosts name this Merchant2).

3. Open this **Merchant** folder on the server - you will be transferring files into this folder.

4. Upload all of the .mvc files into this directory (don't upload the other folders yet).

5. Upload the entire **modules** folder.

6. Some FTP programs let you "drag and drop" files. If yours does not, you will need to create each of the subfolders and upload the proper files to each folder.

7. Upload the entire **lib** folder.

8. Upload the entire **graphics** folder.

Installing via the .tar File

The .tar file can extract on the server and create all the directories for you.

STEP BY STEP

1. In the **HTML** directory (where your index.html file is located), upload the .tar file in BINARY mode.

2. Connect via telnet to your server (see your hosting provider's instructions for this).

3. Navigate to the root directory which contains the .tar file.

4. Type the command: `tar -xvf filename` (the name of the .tar file) and press enter. The files will all extract to the proper directories.

Miva Merchant Setup

The Miva Merchant setup process will initialize the files on the server so you are able to create and configure your online store.

Usually, the setup file, setup.mvc is located in one of two places on your domain:

http://www.yourdomain.com/Merchant/setup.mvc
http://www.yourdomain.com/cgi-bin/miva?Merchant/setup.mvc

Your directory names may differ. If you are unsure, check with your host or server technician.

STEP BY STEP

1. Run the setup.mvc file (at your domain address – as above).

2. Accept the License Agreement.

3. Follow the on-screen instructions.

    Enter the proper URL (web addresses) and the absolute paths (directories) for Miva Merchant, the modules, and the graphics. Miva Merchant's setup will detect the domain and offer a default choice for you. Usually the default information on this screen is correct, providing there have been no special installations. If you are not sure if these are correct, you need to check with your hosting provider to confirm these directories.

    If SSL is not yet configured for the domain, leave of the "s." This can always be updated later.

    The Root directories are usually just /Merchant/ (or /Merchant2/, etc.).

    The mail server is usually something like mail.yourdomain.com or localhost. You may need to check with the host about this.

    When creating the initial username, keep in mind this will be the main administrator. Create a username and password you will remember, but one that others do not know.

Appendix B
Design Basics

Besides creating and maintaining your Miva Merchant store, you will need to provide a home page, and possibly some other pages, for your visitors. Since the merchant.mvc file is not accessed without a link (or a remote forward), you'll need an index page on your site. This page could simply refer (with either a link or an auto-forward command) to the merchant.mvc file.

We'll be discussing some of the basic, yet important issues. We will not, however, go beyond the amount of HTML you need for headers and footers. If you are totally new to Web design and HTML coding, we suggest either finding someone to design these pages for you, or spend some time learning.

Load Time Can Kill You

Load time is the amount of time it takes for a Web page to load. Measured in seconds, the load time of a page determines who stays at your site and who leaves before ever moving past the first lines of text.

If your pages take a long time to load, you will lose customers. There is no argument to this. Someone will be happy to go elsewhere if it takes forever for your site to load.

It is your job to keep load time to a minimum. We cannot stress the importance of this issue, so we'll put it bluntly: **load time has the ability to make or break your online venture**.

Here are the most common issues that contribute to hefty, unnecessary load times on a Web site:

♦ Graphics & Images that are too large in file size

♦ Poorly written or complex cgi scripts

♦ Poor connection

♦ Slow server

♦ Too many processing scripts or applications, such as chatting software and rotating ad scripts, if not configured properly

♦ Scripts that pull information from other servers (if they have delays, you may as well)

The point is, essentially, you have nearly total control over how long your pages take to load. While you can't control someone's Internet connection, you can control which host you use. If your host's servers are slow, talk about this with them. It's possible the server your site is on has been overlooked in the "speed" department.

How Quick Should It Load?

The faster, the better. Ideally, visitors on a 28.8K modem should be able to access your pages within 12 seconds. Pages taking 20 seconds or longer to load lose a good portion of their visitors immediately.

Visitors on hi-speed connections, such as Cable or DSL, should get load times of 2 seconds or less. Three seconds isn't horrible, four is pushing it.

Though this entire tutorial is for Miva Merchant, your site will include a home page, plus other pages you will create with HTML. Pay attention to using proper tags, and methods to keep the load time to a minimum.

Don't Assume...

Don't assume that all visitors are using a cable or DSL modem and the latest browsers. There are still many surfers on a 14.4K, Windows 3.1 and Netscape 2.0. It's likely, now, that they may fail to see a few layouts exactly as you wish, but they should be able to view every image, read every line of text, and access most features of your site.

Test Frequently

If you plan to just throw up your store and site, then just walk away so it can run on its own, don't expect to make a living with your online store. A good designer or company will constantly test their sites to make sure the layout and design is pleasing to the eye, easy to navigate, and loads quickly (we'll have this hammered in by the end of this section).

There are utilities you can use to test your sites compatibility with load times, available browsers and HTML. Use them.

In short:
Test your site often. Love testing your site. Learn to make testing your site a daily ritual.

Resolutions & Window Sizes

Miva Merchant creates pages of your categories and products dynamically, and the pages will be viewed in width and height according to the **resolution** a visitor's computer is set to use. You can specify how wide the pages are, but the resolution actually depicts how it is displayed to the individual visitor.

The resolution is the number of **pixels** the monitor will display. Images and web page widths are not measured in inches.

Essentially, a 14-inch monitor will display 640 pixels wide by 480 pixels high. A 15-inch monitor will usually display both the 640 x 480 plus 800 x 600 (the user can select their resolution). Most 17-inch monitors will display 640 x 480, 800 x 600, 1024 x 768 and some even higher.

What happens when a site designed for 1024 x 768 is viewed on a 14-inch monitor? Chances are the visitor has to scroll from left to right in order to view the entire page. This is yet another setback many designers face.

Generally, most visitors can view at 800 x 600, but again, **we don't assume**. Thus, to make sure *all* visitors can access your site without having to scroll from side to side, you have two options:

Size your HTML pages to 595 pixels (or relative) wide.
You can use tables to do this.

> **- OR -**

Make your HTML pages size according to the resolution.
If you visit a site like **www.amazon.com**, you'll find that if you shrink your browser window or change resolutions, you can still see the entire width of the pages, however, you may have longer pages, since less text can be displayed on each line. But you never have to scroll left and right (unless you shrink your browser down so small you wouldn't appreciate the pages anyway).

Many designers now size for an 800 x 600 pixels wide (usually setting the width to 790 or so). This isn't horrible, you just need to keep in mind that even those viewing at 800 x 600 might be using Accessibility Options in Microsoft Windows to display every larger on the screen.

Testing Different Resolutions

Just like you should test your pages with more than one browser, you should also test them at different resolutions.

In Microsoft Windows 95 and higher, you this by right-clicking on the desktop and choosing **Properties**. Click on the **Settings** tab, then select various screen sizes.

Changing resolution on a Macintosh varies according to the version of the operation system. Latest machines include the ability to change the resolution right from the desktop. Older machines include control panels that will allow these settings to be changed. Check the owners manual for this information.

Images & Custom Graphics

Obviously your store will include images of your products, and you'll likely want to include custom graphics (for buttons, headers, etc.). One of the biggest mistakes a web designer can make is to use images that are too large in either pixel size or file size.

Get a Graphics Program

You can scan till your heart's content, but if you don't have a decent graphics program, you're stuck. Using a program like FrontPage to size your images is not only bad habit, it's unprofessional. As well, most $39.99 programs usually give you what you pay for.

If you only have a few images, or would rather have someone else manipulate images for you, then, by all means, hire someone. If you want to do it yourself, get a decent program. While Photoshop is one of the top choices, it is also expensive (about $600), but other, less expensive programs like PhotoPaint and ImageReady can also do the trick.

Do not rely on your scanning software alone to create awesome images for you. They seldom do.

Scan it the Right Way

Here's where there's a lot of confusion and argument. Many scanners come with software that screams "anyone can do it!" Well, essentially, this is true. Just about anyone can and will scan images on even a $29 scanner, and actually get a decent scan. However, the way you scan and the file types you use are key.

Scan Resolution

Most scanners are versatile in the resolution and size settings. The myth among the ill-informed that the higher resolution you scan at the better the picture will look frustrates visitors and designers. While scanning at 300 dots per inch (dpi) will allow your image to look great on printed paper, it won't make a noticeable difference when viewed on a Web site—monitors are designed to display at a default of 72 dpi.

If you want to cram an image at 200 dpi into your Web page, go right ahead. All it will do is increase the file size and, in turn, load time of the page.

Also, unless you really know what you are doing, scanning at a high resolution then just dropping the image down to 72 dpi will produce a less clear image than if you scanned at the lower resolution itself. Thus, you should scan for the screen.

 There are arguments that images can even be displayed at lower than 72 dpi, while this is essentially true, there are many other factors to consider, including printing pages where one can at least make out the images. The Web standard is 72 dpi.

Scan Size

Okay, we talked about the users who are still viewing at a resolution of 640 x 480. Keep this in mind when scanning and sizing your images. Since the Miva Merchant Look and Feel includes category listings on the left, that is called-for space (it's why we said to keep your category names short). This leaves about 300-425 pixels left on the right side for your image if you are sizing for everyone.

You may not be using the category tree, or you may add a right-hand column. You need to take any called-for space into consideration.

We recommend keeping your full-sized product images at or below 300 pixels wide. We've found that 225 pixels wide is usually ideal for a product image. If you need to show off more detail, you can always link to a larger image in a new window.

File Types

Most image programs let you save your images in either one or many file formats. The most common are:

JPG – used scanned images (such as photos) for clarity and file size.

GIF – used for computer-generated graphics (text buttons, etc.) for file size

TIF – when for the Web, used as a base image, which will be manipulated in your graphics program, then converted to either JPG or GIF

If you've got the knowledge and the software, we recommend scanning images as a TIF, then converting to JPG in your graphics program. Why? Because when you save a TIF, make changes, then save again, you are not compromising clarity of the file.

The JPG format uses a compression process. When you save a JPG, then open it, make changes and save again, then again… you are compromising the clarity of the file. Try it, you'll see that the more you change and save, or size and save, the fuzzier the image gets.

Now, here's the tricky part about JPG vs. GIF. If you scan an image, after making changes, make it a JPG. If you make it a GIF, the file could be dithered, and the file size will be larger than that of a JPG. The only time you make a scanned image a GIF is if it is line art or a hard-edged logo.

If you create an image solely on the computer, make it a GIF. If you make it a JPG, the file size will likely be larger.

So, that's JPG for scans and GIF for computer-created images and line art. But, there's one other factor – AOL.

In past years America OnLine (AOL) users could count for up to 60% (or more) of your traffic, depending on how your site was found (search engines) and your target audience. With the launch of more Internet providers, this number has likely dropped for most sites, but AOL users still take up a significant amount of the pie. Some versions of AOL uses a JPG compression in their program settings, and, believe it or not, most AOL 4.0 or lower users are used to seeing grainy or fuzzy images on the Web, unless they know how to change the settings in their AOL software. Thus, another reason to use the GIF format for your computer-generated graphics.

AOL's settings have gotten a thousand percent better over the years, but designers still find issues. You can get information on AOL issues in regard to web surfing to assist in your design at http://webmaster.info.aol.com/

Those Digital Cameras

If you are planning to use a digital camera to shoot your products, keep a few things in mind:

Clarity is important. Chances are that $49 camera is not suitable for product images. Do a search for reviews at epinions.com or zdnet.com and buy a camera that will serve the purpose. You want crisp, clean images you can manipulate if need be.

Lighting, lighting. Don't snap pictures in your kitchen with a 100 watt light bulb. Find a very "white" area, use white light and shoot clean. You don't have to spend a lot of money, either. Taping a clean white sheet in the corner of the living room, and shining industrial lights or halogens at it can work wonders.

Surfing Overload. The file size initially produced will still be too large for your site. You will still need to manipulate file sizes.

Digital cameras are an excellent tool for your site, but read the manuals and join user groups for their use… you'll be producing top-notch images that can load fast in no time.

Fonts Galore

There's a lot of talk about graphics when it comes to the Miva Merchant store, but not much about fonts. If you're set on producing a great looking store, pay attention to the fonts you use.

We'll make it clear up front: if you plan to use any of those fancy fonts you installed on your system because they just look so cool, forget them. **We've found some fancy ones ourselves, but can never use them for the default fonts for *any* web site...**

They're all some pretty neat typestyles – and we've got more than 2,000 of them, adding more every week. But never, *ever*, use them as text fonts for your site. Such fonts should ONLY be used in images and graphics for the site.

Don't believe us? Read on...

To Use or Not To Use

Ah, the never-ending question amongst those in the beginning learning stages of web site design.

Essentially, there are only six base fonts that should be called in any HTML file. They are:

Times – Times New Roman

Arial – Helvetica

Tahoma - Verdana

Times New Roman is called by PC users; Times is called by MAC users. Arial is PC; Helvetica is MAC. Verdana and Tahoma are PC.

The "Times" fonts are standard on nearly very computer. So is "Arial" and "Helvetica." The "Verdana" and "Tahoma" fonts were introduced in the past few years to PC users, and have become a standard for many sites.

> *There's also a fallback typestyle of sans-serif to be used in conjunction with the Arial and Helvetica fonts.*

Thus, if you want to use other typestyles, consider using them only as heading graphics.

Here's some common pitfalls of new web-builders, or, those who want to do it all themselves but aren't sure how to do it…

It hurts my eyes! Believe it or not, sites that use any non-standard font as it's default text is creating a cumbersome read. The font might be the best looking ever, but if it's not one we're used to reading, we can't handle it.

My Default Display… Consider this. That awesome font you're calling isn't installcd on our machines, so guess what we see? A default font set by our browser… which could be a Times, Arial or Tahoma family font.

Journalism 101. There's a reason the standard styles for newspapers hasn't changed in centuries. We can read the pages! Every newspaper uses a serif font for it's standard text. Why? Because it flows well… we can read it! It's the same type of font we see in books.

Assigning Fonts

As any font not installed on the visitor's computer will not be viewed, we want to make sure the site will look as close as possible to our customers as we see it. If we don't follow proper assignments, the browser's default font is used. This is why we use the multiple font face tag.

<FONT FACE="Arial, Helvetica, sans-serif">

This tells the browser that if the Arial font is not installed, display the Helvetica font. That's perfect, because nearly all PCs have the Arial font and nearly all MACs have the Helvetica font. A fall back is simply sans-serif.

<FONT FACE="Tahoma, Verdana, Arial, Helvetica">

This tells the browser that if the Tahoma font is not installed, display Verdana; if the Verdana font is not installed, display Arial; and if Arial is not installed, display Helvetica. We've pretty much covered our bases here.

<FONT FACE="Times, Times New Roman">

This tells the browser that if the Times font is not installed, display Times New Roman.

When assigning fonts, always place the favored font first. The browser will search each, from left to right.

Using Font Tags

If you supply no font tags, then the browser's default font will be displayed (usually Times or Times New Roman).

Font tags must be closed with </FONT>, and reside around the text they are assigned to. Example:

<FONT FACE="Arial, Helvetica">This is the text inside the tag.</FONT>

The tags are used for the HTML files you may create. In the Miva Merchant admin area, you will just enter the names of the fonts, separated by commas.

Font Sizes

The font size also plays a large role. The larger the font, the easier it may be to read, but you need to also consider the layout of the pages.

By default, Miva Merchant assigns a size of –2 to the Category Tree fonts.

-2 is about this small

Can you read that with little to no effort? If so, then your eye doctor probably despises you because you won't be spending lots of money on glasses this year.

A generic font size for fonts like Arial, Helvetica and Verdana is –1.

-1 is about this size

That's a little better, and usually adequate for lists of information and short paragraphs.

While many sites implement the –1 size, they have decided to use a +1 size for the Category Tree.

+1 is about this size

This is a larger size, and just about anyone should be able to read it with no problems.

The font size tag looks like this:

<FONT SIZE="-1">

Or, you can combine it with the font face tag:

<FONT FACE="Times, Times New Roman" SIZE="+1">This is the text inside the Font tag.</FONT>

Keep in mind, however, that with the Category Tree, the larger the font size, the more room the tree takes on the page.

Basically, if you only have a handful of categories, you can use +1 as a size. Otherwise, you should use –1 for long listings.

For additional information on font sizes and how they affect your HTML pages, you should visit the Web Developer's Virtual Library, an HTML standards and tutorial site, at **www.wdvl.com**.

Colors

There are two very important lessons to learn about colors. The first is, colors work together based on their values. The second is, not every computer displays colors the same way, which is why you should be sure to use hexadecimal values and web-based colors instead of other methods (such as RGB values or pantone color charting).

If you don't have an eye for color (believe it or not, most people don't), you should use resources to determine the best color schemes. There are many resources on the World Wide Web that can assist you.

Browser Safe Colors

Not all colors (there are millions) are browser safe. Sadly, the availability of web-safe colors is pretty minimal (there's only 216), which makes it pretty cumbersome. Fortunately, those color values provide consistent results on monitors that display at 256 colors and above. Since most users have monitors that display millions of colors, there is more flexibility.

If you use colors that are not designed for 256 monitors, then results on monitors set to only display 256 colors will provide skewed results. Monitors will adjust the colors, whereas a light grey color on your monitor might look an ugly green on someone else's screen.

Using browser safe colors eliminates dithering on older machines. Dithering is the process a monitor performs when it can't display a native color—it instead tries to match it to the best color available. That's why photographs may look very grainy on older monitors.

While most newer machines resort to 16.7 million colors during the setup process, some still resort to 256, depending on the graphics card, configuration and monitor. Many new users don't realize they can change this.

So What Do You Do?
There's a great deal of debate. Most Web site owners say they don't care—that the number of these "old ways" users is so minimal it doesn't matter. Others say to stick with browser safe colors. A lot of it depends on your target audience as well.

It is recommended that you use browser safe colors for your fonts and links.

Browser safe colors are defined by a hexadecimal value (which is based on a 16 numbering system). You can find charts of all browser-safe colors (using hexadecimal values) on the Web. A good starting point is **www.wdvl.com**.

The Very, Very Basics of HTML

If you're planning to really *design* your own pages, then look no further. Run to the bookstore and pickup an HTML manual. You'll need to learn the language.

Here we provide just a handful of tags you can use when creating your headers and footers for your Miva Merchant Store. These are standard tags and require no special coding.

We've already learned the FONT tags in the previous section. That was the hard part.

All tags explained here use an open and end tag. This means once you use the opening tag, you need to include another tag (the same with a /) to close the tag.

The following table outlines the basic tags you can use in your headers, footers and store welcome message.

ACTION	OPEN TAG	CLOSE TAG	EXAMPLE
BOLD	\<B>	\</B>	\<B>Bold The Text\</B>
ITALIC	\<I>	\</I>	\<I>Italicize The Text\</I>
UNDERLINE	\<U>	\</U>	\<U>Underline The Text\</U>
CENTER	\<CENTER>	\</CENTER>	\<CENTER>Centers Text\</CENTER>
PARAGRAPH	\<P>	\</P>	\<P>This is paragraph one.\</P>
			\<P>This is paragraph two.\</P>
LINE BREAK	\ 	NONE	This is the text on line one.\ This text is on very next line (no paragraph).
EXTRA SPACE	\	NONE	This is a command to put extra spaces between words. By default, HTML reads ONE space between words, even if you hit the space key several times.

Referencing Other Files

You may want to reference other HTML files, or other store pages, that explain store procedures. These files might include ship cost information, pricing, privacy issues and contact information. If you have actual HTML files for these, they most likely end with a .html or .htm file extension.

The HREF tag is used to reference these files.

<A HREF="shipping.html">Read Shipping Info</A>

This tag will look in the /Merchant/ directory for a file called shipping.html

Notice that the <A HREF= calls the file name, and then closes with >. After the text you want linked is typed, the closing tag is </A>.

If the file is located somewhere else, you'll need to put the location in the tag.

<A HREF="www.yourdomain.com/about.html">About Our Company</A>
<A HREF="../about.html">Read Shipping Info</A>

Either one of these will result in a link labeled "About Our Company," and will take the visitor to the about.html page in the base directory on the domain.

A note, however, that the second example above (using ../) will be called relatively, so if the visitor is currently in SSL mode, it will call that link in secure mode.

Inserting Images

If you want to call in graphics or product images, you'll need to use IMG tag. You will also need to know the location of the file.

<IMG SRC="image.jpg">

This tells the file to look in the current directory (such as /Merchant/) for the file image.jpg.

Chances are, however, your images will be located elsewhere, such as on your domain (in no folder), in a folder on your domain, or in the graphics/00000001 directory (for product images).

<IMG SRC="http://www.yourdomain.com/logo.gif">

This calls the logo.gif file from the base directory on the domain.

<IMG SRC="graphics/00000001/image01.jpg">

This calls a specific image from the /Merchant/graphics/00000001/ directory as a relative link. This is the format you'll use when calling images in headers and footers in the store. Notice that we didn't include the /Merchant/ directory – because we are already in that directory.

Use the ALT and other tags
When referencing images you should always use three other tags.

ALT—the name of the image, or a description of it. This helps with search engines and helps visitors know descriptions of the image. If it's a button, it tells them what will happen if they click on it.

HEIGHT—denotes the height, in pixels, of the image.

WIDTH—denotes the width, in pixels, of the image.

Signifying the height and width help align the page before the images load.

You're final image call should look like this:

<IMG SRC="graphics/00000001/image01.jpg" ALT="John Deere Riding Lawn Mower – Now on Sale" HEIGHT="65" WIDTH="175">

Hyperlinking Images

You can make images link to other files or product pages using both the IMG and the HREF tags.

<A HREF="http://www.yourdomain.com"><IMG SRC="graphics/00000001/logo.gif" ALT="Cindy's Candy Store – click for home page" HEIGHT="42" WIDTH="165" BORDER="0"></a>

The additional BORDER tag tells the browser not to put a hyperlink border around the logo.

Using the HREF and IMG tags together is the same as using them alone. The IMG tag is inside the HREF tags, just as text could also be there.

Referencing Your Store

You can link to your own store by using the HREF tag:

<A HREF="http://www.yoursite.com/Merchant/merchant.mvc">Enter the Store</A>

Or, you can reference a product page. Just put the URL in the tagline above.

Don't worry if the tag runs over lines or looks like it's broken apart. It will be fine.

Automating HTML

There are many HTML editors that will let you click your way to creating links and image calls, as well as handling font tags, etc. We do not recommend FrontPage, as it tends to place tremendous amounts of unnecessary code in the files. It also requires the host has FrontPage extensions installed on the server. Only seasoned designers should be using FrontPage, saving files as straight HTML.

Other programs include **WYSIWYG** (What You See Is What You Get – pronounced wizzywig) features. These can be useful for creating complete pages and generating tables that flow elements together nicely. These programs include Dreamweaver and HomeSite.

Or, you can get a point and click editor that will build the code, which you can then preview in the browser. These types of editors are ideal because, although they require more training for the end user, they produced the cleanest possible HTML code. Our best pick? **Note Tab** and **NoteTab Light**—the light version is free, but the standard version includes additional key features, most importantly a spell checker. These programs can be found at **www.notetab.com**.

Cascading Style Sheets (CSS)

When CSS was introduced, many designers fell in love with the concept. It saved a ton of work and allowed the update of how elements like fonts, tables and paragraphs are displayed in one simple step. The only problem was, it had to be supported by the browser. Today, CSS are a standard. While it is not available to 100% of all Web surfers (such as those running old, old browsers and some proprietary programs), it is acceptable now to use it even in e-commerce sites.

Miva Merchant does not have built-in support for CSS. The only way for it truly to be done is to strip out all the standard font calls from the core script files and build in additional code support. However, CSS has been very successful with just a few steps.

By installing a third-party module that allows you to place additional code between the <HEAD> tags (which are created by Miva Merchant), you can call in a style sheet. You can then remove all the font names and sizes from the Fonts list in the Miva Merchant Admin. When doing this, make sure to upload your .css file to a the /Merchant/ directory so it can be called relatively.

 Some third-party modules that call fonts may override your CSS, so you may need to strip the fields there, as well.

Is this process 100% foolproof? No. However, many Miva Merchant stores using properly formatted CSS have tested successfully on Netscape versions 4.7 and higher and Internet Explorer 4.0 and higher, as well as many other alternative browsers.

To learn about CSS, we suggest you visit **www.wdvl.com**

Flash

It's neat, fun, and classy. Right? Not necessarily. While Flash presentations can be pretty cool, they do not belong on 95% of the e-commerce sites out there. The only time you should consider incorporating Flash with an online store is if the target audience is completely hi-tech.

Problems with Flash in E-commerce Sites

Clunky presentations—unless you have created a high-end, cutting edge presentation, a Flash presentation may actually take away from your site.

Latest Versions—if the presentation requires the latest version of the Flash Player, visitors may be prompted to download a new version. Sorry, but no one should have to download software in order to visit your store.

Load Time—those folks in the sticks may not appreciate having to wait for the presentation to load, and may not notice the skip intro button (if you even created one). This is even more frustrating when Flash has been implemented in the store pages themselves.

Let 'Em Surf at Their Own Speed—some presentations move along too quickly, meaning some of your visitors might miss the entire message.

Some e-commerce sites welcome visitors with a Flash intro on the home page, while others incorporate flash right into the shopping experience. The problem is, it is not for everyone.

If your target audience is techies who are running the latest computers and software, then go for it. Otherwise, anything requiring the Flash Player should be an add-on, prompted with a link to click on only if the potential customer wants to view the presentation.

Appendix C
Payment Gateways

In order to accept credit cards at your online store, you need to have a merchant account. You may also *choose* to have charges approved real-time (as orders are placed), instead of manually processing credit card charges yourself. For this you need a payment gateway.

If you are planning to process all charges yourself, offline, you do not need a payment gateway. Payment gateways are services offered aside from a merchant account, so they carry their own fees.

Miva Merchant comes with various modules to work with several payment gateways. You are not required to use any of these payment gateway companies. Other companies are available. However, at this time, these are the only ones supported by Miva Merchant Modules which are packaged with the store license. Gateways for other services would need to be purchased from third-party developers or developed from ground up (which can be very expensive).

The following gateways are supported in Miva Merchant version 4.23. Not all are available in prior versions.

PayQuake	eValuCheck
PayPal	Moneris e-SELECT
Miva Payment	debit-it!
U.S. Merchant Systems	Verisign Payflow Pro
Rodopi	Verisign Payflow Link
E-Commerce Exchange/QuickCommerce 3.0	Cardservice/LinkPoint
Paradata, Innovative	CyberSource ICSv2
GlobalCommerce	CyberCash, Authorize.Net

If you do not yet have a merchant account, then there are other things to consider. Some merchant account providers will only work with specific gateways, while some offer their own gateway. For example, Miva Payment provides both the merchant account and the gateway.

Ideally, you want to choose the best merchant account for your needs, and the best evaluated payment gateway. This will provide the best overall solution.

PayPal itself does not offer merchant accounts. However, customers can pay you with a credit card or as a draft from a checking or savings account, so it is considered as a payment gateway. You will use only one merchant account and gateway for that account in your store, but you can also use PayPal as an additional payment method.

AUTHORIZE .NET

Setting Up the Payment Gateway

The setup for each payment gateway is different, as each requires specific information. They all require that you provide information that identifies you—such as a username or login ID, and a password.

You must already have signed up with a payment gateway in order for it to work in Miva Merchant.

To setup the gateway in Miva Merchant:

1. In the Admin Menu, click the ▶ next to your store name's link.

2. Click the **Payment Configuration** link.

3. Check off the payment gateway you will use.

4. Click the **Update** button.

5. At the top of the screen, the payment gateway you just activated will be listed as a link. Click the link for the payment gateway.

6. Enter all necessary fields.

7. Click the **Update** button.

For assistance on what to complete in any specific fields, click the ⬛ button in the top right-hand corner of the screen. You'll also find additional references for gateway configurations and the MvCommerce.net Web site.

Testing the Gateway

Many of the payment gateways have a test mode that is either activated in your terminal with that service provider, or from within the Miva Merchant Admin. It is recommended that you place test orders with each credit card type you accept to make sure the payment gateway is working. After placing a successful order, visit your gateway's Web terminal to make sure the authorization and/or sale took place.

Troubleshooting the Gateway

If you are unable to place a successful test order, there may be problems with either the gateway, the server configuration or the configuration of the gateway's module in Miva Merchant.

Payment gateways may require that specific **commerce libraries** be installed on the server and that your domain has permission to use them. If you receive an error that denotes and unsupported commerce method, check with your host, as the proper commerce library may not be installed. These libraries are distributed with Miva Empresa – the engine that lets Miva Script run on the server.

Errors that refer to an unauthorized user usually signify that a wrong login or password was used in the configuration of the module.

Payment type errors usually signify that the merchant account is not configured to accept the credit card type the customer selected. Make sure you did not check off any credit card types you do not accept.

Various other errors can occur, and some are a result of the gateway service itself. When you utilize a gateway, the actual module installed in Miva Merchant works with the gateway to handshake between your Miva Merchant store, the gateway service and the merchant account. Thus, your online store is relying on a few different factors, including the processing of specific card types. If any error occurs after your online store has been running successfully, you would need to contact your host or your gateway provider.

Appendix D
The KoolCat Look and Feel

Most new stores KoolCat Look and Feel—it's an antiquated design that most third-party developers don't even support. Miva Corp. continues to support its initial design and functions for the sake of those who initially used it back in version 1.x.

Many new users checkout this look and feel out of curiosity. If you have not yet setup your Miva Merchant store with headers and footers and other parameters, feel free to take a look. However, if you have already built elements of your store, **take note that switching to this look and feel now will wipe out all the settings**, including any headers and footers and other custom messages. Hopefully the images in this section will suppress your desire to do so.

If you plan to implement this Look and Feel, you'll need to take note of some different features (and lack thereof) from the Miva Merchant Look and Feel.

 Any time you change the Look and Feel for your store, you will lose settings, unless you have backed up all the files or use a third-party module that will backup your settings! Always make a backup of all your files (on the server) in case you want to change back.

The Look and Feel in a Nutshell

The KoolCat Look and Feel is very basic, and requires customers to select to either Browse or Search the catalog.

When using the KoolCat Look and Feel, he first page of the Miva Merchant store will be a directory, offering the options to only browse, search or become an affiliate (if the affiliate program is enabled). It doesn't leave much room for running a customer-friendly online store.

The navigation is completely a click-to and click-back, which means customers have to click on Browse, click on a category, and to get back to the main menu or view other categories, click a back button.

Categories & Products

The KoolCat Look and Feel uses categories as with the Miva Merchant Look and Feel. However, attributes are not displayed on the product pages—the customer is instead prompted with attributes and options after attempting to add the item to the basket.

Also, the standard layout features are not the same, as shown here.

Instead of a listing of products on the category screen, KoolCat lists the items in a table, and includes the product thumbnail, price and a Buy 1 Now link. The customer has to click on the thumbnail or product name in order to access the product information and quantity button.

KoolCat Administration

The administration area for the KoolCat Look and Feel is similar to that for the Miva Merchant Look and Feel. Basically, you can include the same features, such as customer accounts and price groups.

However, there are various features not available and the way KoolCat handles **Headers and Footers** is different.

Instead of entering the **Header and Footer** information in the administration area, you need to create files Miva Merchant will call. These are HTML files that will include your header/footer information.

For example, if you want to place a header on the Catalog Main Page, you need to create an HTML file (you can name it catmain.html). Then you need to place this HTML file in a directory on your server.

In the Header line (shown above), you'll type the full URL to the file (i.e. http://www.yoursite.com/Merchant2/catmain.html), then select **GET** as the command. This will take the catmain.html file and place all the information in the header for the Category Main Page.

The DO command allows you to reference a directory from the root of the server; the POST allows you to run advanced operations. Chances are you won't use either of these at this time, and the operations go beyond the scope of this tutorial.

Appendix E
Miva Merchant Wizards

Miva Merchant introduced Wizards as a means to help even the most novice users click their way to building an online store. It was a great and necessary selling point, because it made it possible for anyone with a computer to just click a mouse and type some words. The only problem is, the Wizards make it too easy for the building of the store, which means some people are using an application they don't really understand.

In Microsoft Word, we know we can click the **B** button on the toolbar to bold our text (us savvy keyboard operators use CTRL+B to do this). But what if we want to product strike-through text, or subscripts? Unless we know the long way around (Format... Font on the menu), we have to research or ask someone what to do. It's a time waster—we want to do something right now, and we're sitting here waiting for answers. It also means we have little capability of troubleshooting any problems that may arise.

Don't get us wrong, Wizards can be useful tools, especially if you have a co-worker who only needs to setup products or categories for you with little to no experience. We just want to make it clear that relying on them as the sole means of administering the store leaves little room for gaining true knowledge.

This section provides instructions for invoking Miva Merchant Wizards to carry out simple tasks.

Simple Administration Mode...

Miva Merchant includes two administration modes. Throughout the tutorial, we did everything in the Advanced mode. We did it the long way so we could understand HOW Miva Merchant works rather than just how to perform the mere basic tasks.

If you are currently in Advanced Administration mode, click the **Switch to Simple Administration** link at the bottom of the Admin Menu.

The **Simple Administration Mode** utilizes **Wizards** to move you through the initial tasks of building your store.

However, if you initially created your store via the Advanced Administration mode, you will not be able to use the Wizards by way of the Simple Administration mode. Not to worry, though. All the Wizards are also accessible in the Advanced mode. For this reason, to make sure everyone is able to follow our steps, **click back to the Advanced Administration mode**.

Setting Store Properties

After creating the store, you will be able to make changes and add items by using Wizards.

There are two locations in Advanced Administration mode from which you can utilize Wizards. The first is in the main screen—the first screen loaded when you log into the Admin Area. (If you are currently at a different screen, click the MAIN link in the Admin Menu to return to the main screen.). The second is the Wizards menu for your store.

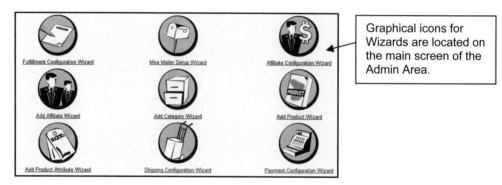

Graphical icons for Wizards are located on the main screen of the Admin Area.

Since it's easier to use the Admin Menu (it stays there as you move around) we'll use the Wizards menu to work with Wizards.

Locating Wizards

There are actually two Wizards links listed in the Admin Menu. The first occurrence is for the mall and is used for creating a store. The second is for the actual store.

STEP BY STEP

---

1. In the Admin Menu, click the ▶ next to Stores.

2. Click the ▶ next to your store name's link.

3. Click the ▶ next to Wizards.

Look & Feel Configuration Wizard

This Wizard provides some basic template designs for your store. Keep in mind that since these designs are a standard in Miva Merchant, many other stores are also using them. If you want to be unique, you really should be implementing a unique design. There are many third-party modules available that will enhance the Look & Feel of your store.

STEP BY STEP

1. In the Admin Menu, beneath **Wizards**, click the **Look & Feel Configuration Wizard** image or link. A new window will open.

2. Click the **Next** button.

3. Select any of the four template designs shown, or opt to keep the current settings (how your store looks right now).

4. Click the **Next** button.

5. If you want to create the store's welcome message, click the **Build Introductory Message** button. Otherwise, click **Next**.

6. You can opt to build categories and products right in this Wizard. If you want to do so, go ahead, otherwise click the Finish button.

You should now view the front end of your store to see the changes. Remember to first refresh the page. The color scheme and navigation buttons will follow the template. No other changes will be apparent here.

Shipping Configuration Wizard

This Wizard will assist you in setting up the proper shipping methods and a means to configure the cost of shipping. You can have more than one shipping method assigned to your store.

You may find the Shipping Configuration Wizard to be a great learning tutorial to better understand how shipping is configured for weight, price and table methods. You could create a few methods here, then see how they are setup under Shipping Configuration in the Admin Area to get a better grasp on how to setup additional methods.

Some previous versions of Miva Merchant included Deutsche shipping methods for German users. They are not covered here.

STEP BY STEP

1. In the Admin Menu, beneath **Wizards**, click the **Shipping Configuration Wizard** image or link. A new window will open.

2. Select the Shipping module you want to use, then click **Next**.

3. Follow the on-screen instructions for configuring shipping.

Restart | Close

Welcome to the Miva Merchant Shipping Configuration Wizard. This wizard allows you to add shipping options that will be offered to your customers.

Miva Merchant calculates shipping costs using a *Shipping Module*. Some shipping modules support services offered by a third-party company, and some shipping modules calculate shipping costs based on a formula you specify.

Some *Shipping Modules* offer pre-configured *Shipping Methods*. These methods configure a shipping module to offer a particular option to your customers.

In the options below, items prefixed with **Module:** indicate a shipping module, and items prefixed with **Method:** indicate a pre-configured shipping method.

To begin, please select a shipping module from the list, and click the **Next** button.

Shipping Module/Method: Module: Price Table Based Shipping

Next

Payment Configuration Wizard

The Payment Configuration Wizard helps you either sign up for Miva Payment—merchant account services and payment gateway provided via Miva Corp., or other payment gateways.

STEP BY STEP

1. In the Admin Menu, beneath **Wizards**, click the **Payment Configuration Wizard** link. A new window will open.

2. To signup for Miva Payment, click **Next**. To setup a different payment gateway, click **Other** and select the gateway from the list.

3. Click **Next**.

4. Follow the on-screen instructions for configuring the gateway.

Add Category Wizard

This wizard helps you create categories you will use for product navigation.

✔ Creating categories with the Wizard means you are allowing Miva Merchant to create the Code for the category. The code is an "ID" for the category, and is also needed to be known by you if you plan to upload your products via text import. Be sure to read the initial tutorial to see how to edit the category (if need be) or to add categories manually. If you are new to Miva Merchant, and plan to enter all of your information for products and categories using the Wizards, then don't worry about this at this time.

STEP BY STEP

1. In the Admin Menu, beneath **Wizards**, click the **Add Category Wizard** link. A new window will open.

2. Click the **Next** button.

3. Enter the **Category Name** you want customers to see.

4. Click the **Next** button.

5. If this is a subcategory, then enter the code of the **Parent Category**. Or, click the 🔘 button and select the main category from a list. If it is not a subcategory, just move to the next step.

6. Click the **Next** button.

7. If you want, you can click the Add Products button to start adding products to this category. We'll use the Product Wizard instead in the next exercise.

8. Click **Finish**.

Miva Merchant will create the category code based on the name of the category, using the first letter of each word. In our example, we created the category Western Wear. The category code of WW was automatically assigned. If we crate another category with the same name (for use as a subcategory under a kids category), the category code of WW1 was created.

Add Product Wizard

This wizard walks you through the steps of creating products for your store. The only drawback is that Miva Merchant will auto-create the product code. So, if you want to use existing sku or item numbers or want to code products with an incremented number system, you will not be able to do so using this Wizard.

STEP BY STEP

---

1. In the Admin Menu, beneath **Wizards**, click the **Add Product Wizard** link. A new window will open.

2. Click the **Next** button.

3. Enter the **Product Name** you want customers to see.

4. Click the **Next** button.

5. Enter the **Price**, **Cost** and **Weight** of the product.

   > *You can use the Cost field for discount and other configurations. Refer to Chapter Five for details.*

6. Click the **Next** button.

7. Enter the **Product Description** customers will read. This can include sentences, paragraphs, even HTML.

8. Click the **Next** button.

9. Use the to upload the product and thumbnail images. (See Chapter Five for detailed instructions.)

10. Click the **Next** button.

11. You will want to assign this product to at least one category (you can only assign it to one using this Wizard). Enter the Category Code or click the ⚫ button to select the category.

12. Click the **Next** button.

13. Review the product's Name, Price, Code, Weight and Description. To make any changes, click the **Previous** button continuously to reach the proper screen.

14. To add another product, click the **Add Additional Products** button. Otherwise, click **Finish**.

You can also start adding attributes and options for this product by clicking the **Add Attributes** button. We'll use the Add Product Attribute Wizard to do this in the next section.

Add Product Attribute Wizard

This Wizard lets you assign product attributes and options. If you need a better understanding of attributes and options, be sure to refer to Chapter Five: *Product Attributes*.

As with products and categories added via the Wizards, Miva Merchant will auto-create the attribute and option codes.

STEP BY STEP

1. In the Admin Menu, beneath **Wizards**, click the **Add Product Attribute Wizard** link. A new window will open.

2. Enter the **Product Code** you want to create attributes and options for, or click the 🔍 button to select the product from a list.

3. Click the **Next** button.

4. Choose what type of attribute you want to create. This will be either Multiple Options, Yes/No checkbox, or Text Fields.

5. Click the **Next** button.

6. Enter the Attribute Prompt (the label the customer will see), and upload any image you'd like to be displayed in place of the prompt.

7. Click **Next**.

8. Tell Miva Merchant if an attribute selection is Required. If you are selling items that need more information in order for them to be processed, it is required. If it is just a list add-ons to the product, it is not required. To require the attribute, check the Required box.

9. Click **Next**.

10. If necessary, choose the Attribute Type (Drop-down List, Radio Buttons; Text Field or Text Area), then click **Next**.

11. Follow the on-screen instructions. Based on the type of attribute you chose to create you may be prompted to enter certain information, such as attribute options (for list formats). You'll also be prompted to enter any price and/or cost information.

12. Once you are happy with the attributes and options you created (you'll see them for consideration), click the **Finish** button.

Since Miva Merchant auto-creates the attribute and option codes, you may not want to use this method. If you are using an order processing system that utilizes these codes to determine the actual product ordered, you will need more control. Thus, you should consider adding attributes and options either via the Advanced Administration or by using a third-party import module.

Fulfillment Configuration Wizard

This Wizard configures the merchant and customer email notification modules. These are what signifies if an email is sent to the customer and/or merchant when an order is placed, and what that email includes.

Why aren't other fulfillment modules included?
If you are using any third-party fulfillment modules, they will not be listed unless the developer has taken the steps to make them accessible via the Wizards. Most developers do not do this because most users do not rely on Wizards to configure the entirety of the Miva Merchant store.

The only modules listed here by default are the **Email Merchant Notification** and **Customer Order Confirmation Email**.

To configure either of these using this Wizard:

1. In the Admin Menu, beneath **Wizards**, click the **Fulfillment Configuration Wizard** link. A new window will open.

2. Select one of the module options from the pull-down menu.

3. Click **Next** and follow the on-screen prompts.

Affiliate Configuration Wizard

This Wizard assists you in setting up and maintaining an Affiliate Program.

STEP BY STEP

1. In the Admin Menu, beneath **Wizards**, click the **Affiliate Configuration Wizard** link. A new window will open.

2. Click the **Next** button.

3. Select the **Default Application Status**. This is the status of everyone who signs up – Pending (approval), Approved or Disabled.

4. Click the **Next** button.

5. Enter the Commission calculation amounts. The screen explains each option.

6. Click the **Next** button.

7. Enter the **Link Image** (if you will use one), **Link Text** and the **Terms** of the Program.

8. Click the **Next** button.

9. Click the **Yes** button to setup the Lost Password Recovery address.

10. Enter the email address you want passwords sent FROM. This is usually the store's email address.

11. Click the **Next** button.

12. Enter the **Subject** and **Header** text of the Lost Password Email.

13. Click the **Next** button.

14. Click **Yes** to setup the affiliate email notification. This email can be sent to you or the affiliate, or both.

15. Enter the email address you want the notification sent FROM.

16. Click the **Next** button.

17. Enter the email address you want the notification sent TO.

18. Click the **Next** button.

19. If you want others to receive the message as well (such as yourself if you initially sent it to the affiliate), you can enter the addresses here.

20. Click the **Next** button.

21. Enter the **Subject** and **Header** text of the message. If this is going to the affiliate, you might want to say something like: Thanks for applying… here is the info you submitted.

22. Click the **Next** button.

23. Confirm your entries. You can opt to add affiliates now, or click **Finish**.

Add Affiliate Wizard

This Wizard steps you through adding affiliates. You must have already enacted the Affiliate Program in order to complete these steps.

STEP BY STEP

1. In the Admin Menu, beneath **Wizards**, click the **Add Affiliate Wizard** link. A new window will open.

2. Click the **Next** button.

3. Create a unique login and password for the new affiliate. The login cannot contain spaces or special characters—only letters, numbers, underscores and dashes.

4. Click the **Next** button.

5. Enter the affiliate's email address, then choose the status (Pending, Approved or Rejected).

6. Click the **Next** button.

7. Enter the details about the affiliate, including address, URL, etc.

8. Click the **Next** button.

9. Enter the commission fees for this affiliate. By default, the settings you made for the store will be entered. You can change these or leave them as is.

10. Click the **Next** button.

11. Confirm the information and either add more affiliates or click **Finish**.

Sales Tax Configuration Wizard

This Wizard steps you through configuration sales tax for the store. Miva Merchant also supports VAT calculations.

By default you can only use one tax method.

STEP BY STEP

1. In the Admin Menu, beneath **Wizards**, click the **Sales Tax Configuration Wizard** link. A new window will open.

2. Select the type of tax you need to collect.

3. Click **Next**.

4. Follow the on-screen prompts and provide applicable information.

5. When complete, click **Finish**.

Wizards for Miva Marketplace and Miva Mailer are discussed in Chapter Twelve.

Appendix F
Miva Merchant Logs, Statistics & Notifications

Miva Merchant includes two logging modules that can assist you in obtaining statistics for your online store. Recent versions also will display basic store statistics in the Admin.

Miva Merchant Access Log

The **Miva Merchant Access Log** module logs customers' actions throughout the store, which you can view in a flat file format. With the file you can determine what browsers customers are using, what search terms they use in the store, and their step-by-step actions (such as clicking on products, adding products to the basket, removing products from the basket, etc.) throughout the store.

This type of logging should not be confused with actual server log files, which usually provide statistics on actions throughout an entire Web site. The Miva Merchant Access Log only supplies information about the Miva Merchant store itself. However, it can be helpful in the study of what search terms customers are using, in turn giving you insight on keywords you should be including in product descriptions.

Activating the Logging

To turn on the Miva Merchant Access Log, in your Admin Menu, click the **Logging Configuration** link, check off the **Miva Merchant Access Log** box, and click **Update**.

By default, the name of the file created will be malf.log. You can change this in the Admin by clicking the Access Log link under Logging Configuration, entering a new file name, and clicking Update.

How It Works

Once activated, the module will begin writing actions in the Miva Merchant store to a file named malf.log (or other name you may have given the file). Logging will begin only when the module is activated in the store, so any prior customer actions will not be included.

Getting the Log File

To obtain the log file, you need to FTP to the server and navigate to the store's data directory. For some versions, the file may be located in a log directory.

Reading the File

The malf.log file is a delimited file that can be opened in nearly any text, spreadsheet or database program. When first viewed, it will look like a jumble of various information. Once you study it further, you will see that it shows how visitors moved about the store. Each visitor's movement is also noted by a unique Session_ID number.

To analyze the log file you may need to setup special functions in a database or spreadsheet program.

Resetting the Log File

The malf.log file can get quite large in file size, which may cause problems if your host limits you to the amount of drive space you can use. Since Miva Merchant will always look for the malf.log file, and will create the file if it is not present, you can back up and then remove this file from the server whenever you need to free up some space. You can always keep a backup for future reference.

E-Urchin Logging

Miva Merchant also includes a logging module which interacts with the Urchin reports products. Enabling E-Urchin logging under Logging Configuration will write data to a file format that is readable by the various Urchin products, which offer fully defined stats, including search engine terms and clicks from outside sites that result in sales.

You can get more information about how E-Urchin log files work with Urchin products at **www.urchin.com**.

Miva Merchant Statistics

Miva Merchant version 4.x provides basic statistics on the main screen in the Admin. These statistics will tell you how many visitors have accessed the store, as well as how many orders were placed, along with best sellers.

To view the statistics, in the Admin, click the MAIN button in the navigation bar, or click the **Main** link in the Admin Menu. Depending on store notifications and other features, you may need to scroll down the right-hand screen.

This feature provides the following information:

> **Hits:** How many individual screens have been loaded; a single visitor can log several hits.
> **Visitors**: The number of unique visitors to the store.
> **Orders:** The number of orders placed.
> **Revenue:** The total sales amount of the orders placed.
> **Products Sold:** The total number of products sold in the orders.

> **Best Sellers:** The top five products sold and the quantity of each.

If you have enabled Miva Marketplace, additional statistics will also be displayed.

You can reset the statistics at any time by clicking the Reset Statistics link. This will not remove or alter any orders.

Statistics		Reset Statistics
		Last Reset on: 08/21/2004
Hits:	628	
Visits:	59	
Orders:	14	
Revenue:	178.00	
Products Sold:	14	

Best Sellers	
6 Steel Hearts (5 x 7):	12
Anissa (5x7):	1
Bernie Wrightson Lab Print (Frankenstein) 11 x 15:	1

Miva Marketplace		Reset Marketplace Statistics
		Last Reset On: 05/30/2004
Referrals:	3	
Orders:		
Revenue		

To reset statistics that are displayed in the Main Admin screen, click the Reset link.

Domain Notifications

Miva Merchant, by default, will display domain notifications. These are notifications about Miva Merchant itself and special offers from Miva Corp.

Domain Notifications are automatically served, but you can control how they are delivered, if at all, by clicking the **Domain Notifications** link in the Admin's Main screen. Simply check off the information you'd like to receive, and the timing of delivery.

If you'd like to check for notifications manually, at your own leisure, select Never. Then, in the Admin, click the **Check for New Notifications Now** link.

Display:	☐ Security Alerts
	☐ Software Updates/Upgrades
	☐ Tips & Tricks
	☐ Documentation Updates
	☐ E-Commerce Newsletter
	☐ Special Offers
Check for Notifications:	○ At Every Login
	○ Daily
	○ Weekly
	⊙ Never

Domain Notifications   Check For New Notifications Now

FREE Upgrade to Miva Merchant 5 with Conference 2004 Registration

(Correction applied) Miva Special Pricing, 04 August '04

Miva Conference '04 Update: WHIR New Media Sponsor

Miva Merchant Tips & Tricks - #1

Miva Merchant Tips & Tricks - #2

Documentation Update: "Getting Started as an Online Merchant"

Miva's August Special Pricing Ends Soon!

Miva Merchant Tips & Tricks - #3

To read the article, click the link. The information will appear in a pop-up window. To remove the notification, open the article and click the delete button.

Store Notifications

Miva Merchant will display a pending orders count, along with other information (if provided by third-party support modules), under the **Store Notifications** section in the Main Admin screen. Clicking the link for these will display a pop-up window with the information.

To tell Miva Merchant to remove this notification, click the link to the pop-up and then click the delete button. This will not remove the actual orders from the store, only the notification from the Main screen.

Index

"I want to break out of the box...
without breaking my store..."

Face it. You can't know everything. DesignExtend.com is about solutions. We've helped more than **5,000 customers** get online and stay there. And if we don't have the answer, we'll get one.

We're more than just a module shop. DesignExtend.com is a one-stop community!

Modules & Apps
You'll find hundreds of Miva Merchant add-ons, plus key e-commerce site software and tools.

Training Tools
Learn more about Miva Merchant with books, ebooks, tips & resources, and the weekly email tips.

Services
The DesignExtend.com is comprised of experts in e-commerce development, site design, analysis and consulting - all focused on Miva Merchant.

We even offer publishing services for catalogs and promotions.

Shopping Directory
Support other Miva Merchant stores at a directory just for those who use the best e-commerce software on the market.

Real Profiles
Check out standard and customized online stores we've worked with. You will see the possibilities are endless.

How-Tos
Want to know how it's done? You ask, we answer.

Interaction
The user-to-user message boards help you find the answers you need... right now.

Support
We support every product we sell and every service we offer. And if you just need a little direction on how to perform a task, we'll answer that, too!

Partners
We take our partnerships seriously. We'll never recommend someone until we've worked with the company ourselves. In fact, we'll never carry a product we have not used ourselves.

Real Contacts
We answer our ticket, desk and our phones. Go ahead and leave a message, we *will* get back to you.

Make the BEST of Your Online Store

Ready to compete with the big dogs? This all-new tutorial tells you what makes online stores work. You'll learn how to analyze your Miva Merchant store for usability and shopability.

Written by the author of *E-commerce Made Easy*, this 70+ page ebook is a definitive resource, spotlighting Miva Merchant stores that work and why customers shop them like a breeze.

Available in downloadable PDF format today...at designextend.com

---

Now offering modules & software created by top developers:

Copernicus Business Systems - Viking Coders - Bill Weiland - Santa Fe Mall - truXoft
PhosphorMedia - OpenUI Consortium - StoneEdge - Wump Services

"I need solutions to make my store stand out...
and support for them..."

Need a quote for custom services? Call our sales team at: 305-752-3943

You'll find it all...at DesignExtend.com
A division of Media Services Int'l, Inc. A pourd member of the BBB.

The Stone Edge *Order Manager*
A Complete Back-Office Solution
for Miva Merchant Users

As your business grows, you need systems that will grow with you and help you stay efficient and profitable. The Stone Edge Order Manager is the complete back office solution for Miva Merchant users. *Whether you ship 10 or 2,000 orders per day, the Order Manager has the capabilities you need to manage your operations!*

- ◆ **Supports Web, Manual (phone, fax, email, etc.) and Point-of-Sale Orders**
- ◆ **Fully integrated with Miva Merchant**
  - ➢ Automatic downloading of orders, customers and product information from your Miva store.
  - ➢ Batches new orders automatically before it imports them.
  - ➢ Real-time inventory updates between the Order Manager and Miva Merchant!
  - ➢ Supports popular Miva scripts for coupons, discounts, gift certificates, inventory tracking, etc.
  - ➢ No per-store charges! Includes compiled and uncompiled Miva scripts.
- ◆ **Automates and streamlines many of your daily tasks:**
  - ➢ Automatic address validation!
  - ➢ Tests for "do not ship to" customers, email addresses, IP numbers, etc.
  - ➢ Automatically approves orders, cancels orders or changes shipping methods based on address fields, items ordered, weight or value of order, AVS response, etc.
  - ➢ Automatic credit card processing. Supports Authorize.net, PayflowPro and other gateways.
  - ➢ Sends purchase orders to drop-shippers and orders to fulfillment centers.
  - ➢ Emails order confirmations to your customers.
  - ➢ Updates inventory quantity-on-hand, creating backorders as needed.
- ◆ **Easy handling of backorders, returns, exchanges and other order modifications**
- ◆ **New *Pack & Ship* system!**
  - ➢ Eliminates packing errors! Confirm each item as you pack it, with or without a barcode scanner.
  - ➢ Prints UPS, Fedex and USPS shipping labels!*
  - ➢ Imports tracking numbers, pickup dates and shipping costs automatically!
  - ➢ Sends email confirmations with clickable tracking links to your customers!
  - ➢ Supports multiple boxes per order, partial shipments, pack by order or by product, and much more!
  - ➢ * Requires ShipRush software for printing UPS and Fedex labels. Requires Endicia's DAZzle software for printing USPS labels.
- ◆ **CRM features**
  - ➢ Quickly locate orders by order number, customer name or address, etc.
  - ➢ Easily track packages sent via UPS, Fedex, USPS, etc. without leaving the Order Manager!
  - ➢ Powerful email functions. Send free-form or template-based messages. Includes bulk email capabilities.
  - ➢ Optional Web-based Order Status System dramatically reduces telephone support!
- ◆ **Inventory management**
  - ➢ Track quantity-on-hand down to the attribute level (color, size, style etc.)!
  - ➢ Real-time inventory updates with Miva Merchant!
  - ➢ Automatic purchase order generation for restocking.
  - ➢ Supports Kits, Drop-Ship items, "Always in Stock" items, etc.

Easy integration with credit card gateways, shipping software and QuickBooks
Extensive reporting capabilities – supports standard and custom reports
Multi-User Ready – includes license for up to 5 workstations!
Risk-free 30-day return policy

Take a Quick Tour of the Order Manager at:
http://www.stoneedge. com/quicktour.asp

Streamline the entire process of reviewing, processing and shipping orders!
Reduce staff requirements! Save time and money with every order you ship!

For more information, go to StoneEdge.com or call Stone Edge Technologies at 1-877-StoneWeb.

Extras...
Bonus CD

The Bonus CD included with this book contains a wealth of Miva Merchant and e-commerce goodies and documentation—valued at more than $1,000! Contents of the CD are non-transferable.

Features include:

- ♦ A Licensed copy of the OpenUI (a $40 value) for compiled Miva Merchant 4 (versions 4.14 and higher)

- ♦ Free Miva Merchant modules

- ♦ Demonstration Miva Merchant modules

- ♦ The Unofficial Guide to Miva Mia

- ♦ Interactive PDF Catalog of third-party modules

- ♦ E-commerce resources

   ...and much more!!

How to use the CD

To view and utilize content on the CD, you will need:

- ♦ A copy of Adobe Acrobat 5.0 or higher (available for free download at www.adobe.com)

- ♦ An unzipping utility for module files.

- ♦ A licensed copy of Miva Mia (for some demo modules)

The CD includes a main PDF document that is a complete catalog to the contents of the CD. Use this as a directory. If the directory does not appear upon launch of the CD, browse to the file named **CD_INDEX.pdf**.

Registration Information

The initial purchaser of this book may obtain updated documentation of upcoming versions of Miva Merchant, as well as other special offers, for a period of at least one year. To obtain this documentation at no charge, visit **www.MvCommerce.net** and register using the key code included on the CD.

The key code on the CD is also the license key for installation of the OpenUI (for compiled Miva Merchant only).

The registration number is not transferable. If you purchased this book as used, email author@mvcommerce.net for additional options.